The Indignant Years

Drawing of Calvin Coolidge by M. M. Prechtl

The Indignant Years

Art and Articles from the
Op-Ed Page of The New York Times

Edited by Harrison E. Salisbury
with David Schneiderman

Art Editor and Designer:
Jean-Claude Suarès

Crown Publishers /Arno Press

"Washington's Problem-Solvers" © 1971 by Hannah Arendt.
Abridged and reprinted by permission of Harcourt Brace
Jovanovich, Inc. from "Lying in Politics" in CRISES OF
THE REPUBLIC by Hannah Arendt.

"Someday Us Poor Is Going to Overrule" by Shirley Dalton,
copyright © 1972 by Kathy Kahn from the book HILLBILLY
WOMEN by Kathy Kahn. Reprinted by permission of Doubleday
& Company, Inc.

Library of Congress Cataloging in Publication Data

Salisbury, Harrison Evans, 1908-   comp.
     The indignant years.

     1.   United States—Politics and government—1969-
—Addresses, essays, lectures.   2.   United States—Civilization—
1970-   —Addresses, essays, lectures.   I.   Schneiderman,
David, joint comp.   II.   Suarès, Jean-Claude, joint comp.
III.   New York Times.   IV.   Title.
E839.5.S24   1973   917.3'03'924   73-12222
ISBN   0-517-50584-3
ISBN   0-517-51197-5 (pbk.)
SBN   842-801-030 (text ed.)

Manufactured in the United States of America by Arno Press Inc.

Introduction

By Harrison E. Salisbury

Nowhere has the impact of the technological age, the electronification of communication and McLuhanism taken a toll more deadly than in the free and unlimited exchange and expression of opinion.

The newspapers of the 19th Century provided unparalleled diversity of views. The multiplicity of media — 20 or more papers in New York, eight or ten in Chicago and three or four in every city of size, fiercely opinionated, fiercely partisan, made certain that the widest diversity of ideas was readily available to any citizen who had a penny or two to spend.

Nor did he need spend even a penny. Newspapers were not the only media for free-swinging conflict of ideas. The soapbox orator was a commonplace whether in London's Hyde Park or New York's Union Square. On Sunday they offered a bazaar of ideas, of politics, of polemics. In the days before World War I — and even up to the outbreak of World War II — the hoarse voices of outdoor speakers proclaimed the virtues of free love or anarchism, the perils of Imperialism or Communism. Some would pull Queen Victoria or King George from their thrones. Others would abolish marriage, taxes, enthrone Buddha or inveigh against the Yellow Peril.

The complacent London bobby or New York's finest could hardly care less what the orator said — just so long as no free-for-all broke out.

But as the United States neared the 200th anniversary of its independence, as we approached the three-quarter mark of the 20th Century banality held sway. Gone were the soapboxes of a bygone day. Gone were the multitudes of newspapers, the phalanxes of journals of opinion. Gone was their predecessor the pamphleteer.

No longer did families clamber into the buckboard to drive 20 rough miles for "the speaking" at the county fair or the village courthouse. In an era when pushbuttons gave our fingertips access to every capital of the world it was harder to find an uninhibited forum for the exchange of ideas and opinion than it had been in the time of Ulysses S. Grant.

All this at a moment unique in contemporary times for social conflict and crisis, for dissent and alienation, challenge and change, revolt and disillusion, the Generation Gap, the Credibility Gap, for assault on the Establishment and doubt of traditional value systems.

The Seventies ushered in an age of scepticism. Not one institution of American society escaped reexamination — the Church, the Courts, Congress, the White House, the whole system of government, the Banks, the great Corporations, the Foundations, the Universities, the education system from kindergarten to Graduate School, the Press, the Profit motive, Architecture, Literature, Hair styles and Music. Nothing in society was too profound or too trivial to be put under the magnifying glass of critical analysis.

It was into this era that the Op-Ed page of The New York Times was born, a child of its times, a calculated effort to meet what was perceived as one of the great needs of our times, a place where men and women could express themselves on what was closest to their hearts, strongest in their passions, most fiercely in their principles. The criteria for Op-Ed could not have been more simple: to have something challenging to say and to say it with eloquence.

More than 1,000 Op-Ed pages have come and gone — between 2,000 and 3,000 writers have spoken their words. There is hardly a great name in the United States that has not appeared on Op-Ed. Nor have the U.S. boundaries provided a barrier to Op-Ed expression. Every continent has been represented. There are no Iron Curtains for Op-Ed — no silken curtains, no bamboo curtains. There are no barriers of race, religion, politics, class or condition of servitude. Anonymous prisoners have cried for justice from their cells and great Lords of the Church have spoken in compassion or indignation. Politicians cross swords, statesmen launch trial balloons, generals defend wars, students speak for morality and a mother mourns a son, lost to drugs.

The world of Op-Ed is *the* world. It is a world of pain and pride, of anguish and indignation, of repartee and reportage, of the humble and the great. A 10-year-old youngster pleads for the life of the kangaroo and a nonagenarian calls upon a public figure twenty years his junior to retire "for age."

The world of Op-Ed is a world of comedy and tragedy, laughter and tears, bitter conflict, sunny reminiscence.

More. Op-Ed is a marriage of idea and image, of the artist and the writer, a symbiosis of creative forms.

The union of graphics and letters has been a goal of man from the day of the cave. Primitive stone chislers carved on limestone walls scenes of daily life, hunting, fishing, tribal battles, birth and death and accompanied them with ideographic symbols.

In our time the unity of word and image has become a cliché celebrated in billboards, posters, advertising, neon signs on the Las Vegas strip. Which is by way of saying that there is nothing new in the concept of using pictures to illuminate words or words to illuminate pictures.

But the symbiosis of Op-Ed is new. Art is not employed on Op-Ed to "illustrate," to give the reader a picture of the scene the writer is trying to describe. The image is employed not as a visual aid, a space device for breaking up blocks of type, a means of crystallizing abstract concepts. No. The task of Op-Ed's images is to create an environment which extends and deepens the impact of the word; to provide an ambiance in which the writer may more intensively penetrate his reader's mind; an atmosphere which stimulates imagination; which creates a mood, an emotion, consistent with the ideas, the issues or the experience which the writer is presenting.

Art on Op-Ed sometimes speaks for itself, stands alone as a commentary. But when Art so speaks the image itself speaks without benefit of words. It is not cartoon and if it is caricature then it is caricature in a form which has not previously been known.

Most of the writers who appear on Op-Ed are Americans. Most of the artists are Europeans. If any writer has met any artist it is sheer happenchance. The artists do not draw to specific topic or stated content. They create the atmospherics of the liminal. Before a single word has been read the graphics establish the milieu which the reader is entering. His sensibilities have been heightened, his perceptions sharpened, his emotions prepared for the idea which is about to enter his consciousness.

Why should the writers be Americans, the artists Europeans? This does not seem accidental. The focus of Op-Ed is the U.S.A. This dictates that the bulk of the writing be American. But why artists from Europe? Perhaps, because the perspective of distance enables their imagination to grasp with subtlety and originality the essential ingredients of our chaotic world, essentials lost to those who inhabit a forest too full of trees.

This collection samples the brilliance of Op-Ed, its most happy combinations of word and image, a sampler of the anger and dissent of the era, a cross-section of the way Americans saw their world, themselves and their environment, natural, political and ethical, in a turbulent time.

One last note. The magic of Op-Ed is not parthenogenetic. It is midwifed by a brilliant staff — Editors Herbert Mitgang, John Van Doorn and David Schneiderman and Art Director Jean-Claude Suarès who more than any other individual gave life to the Op-Ed symbiosis.

Nixon Turns to China

By JAMES RESTON

WASHINGTON

WASHINGTON, Feb. 1—President Nixon is now concentrating on his forthcoming visit to China—the great diplomatic experiment of his first term in office. He is working his way through a mountain of briefing papers, studying the transcripts of the Kissinger-Chou En-lai conversations, and quietly putting out the word not to expect too much from this month's spectacular journey.

The history of these postwar summit meetings suggests that this is a prudent warning. The Eisenhower-Khrushchev conference at Geneva, the Johnson-Kosygin session at Glassboro, N. J., and the Kennedy-Khrushchev confrontation at Vienna all produced great expectations and even greater disappointments. Mr. Nixon has gone through all these records too, which helps explain why he is protecting himself now against a let-down at the end of the month.

None of these other summits was prepared with such meticulous care as Mr. Nixon's mission to Peking. He has been working up to this almost from his first few months in the White House, and he has not only been studying the problem, but acting to create a favorable atmosphere for his discussions with the Chinese leaders.

His disclosure of his efforts to reach a negotiated settlement in Vietnam is only the latest of these acts. It was a gamble to publicize Dr. Kissinger's secret negotiations with the Vietnamese Communists, and it irritated Hanoi, but the President wanted Peking to know that he had been trying to reach a compromise settlement before he arrived in the Chinese capital.

Mr. Nixon has already bet quite a lot on this Peking trip. By keeping it secret until the last minute of Dr. Kissinger's first trip to Peking, he irritated the Japanese and the Soviet Union, and undoubtedly helped start the negotiations between Moscow and Tokyo for a closer Japanese-Soviet relationship.

Similarly, he sided with Pakistan against India in the recent war, at least partly to avoid a split with Peking on this issue. Without his spectacular moves toward Peking, it is highly doubtful that Taiwan would have been expelled from the United Nations, and even now other U.S. allies in Asia, particularly South Korea and Thailand, are uneasy over the Nixon-Chou talks.

On balance, then, it would seem that China has already gained a good deal even from the preliminaries to the Peking trip. She has established herself in the U.N., she has reminded Moscow that the days of Chinese isolation are over and that the United States is taking an interest in China and in new security relations in Asia; she has loosened the ties between Washington and Tokyo and between Washington and Taiwan, and she will soon be showing over world-wide television the journey of an American President to the Forbidden City, the Summer Palace, the Great Wall, and the serene beauty of the lakes and mountains that surround Hangchow.

What then, it is asked, can Mr. Nixon hope to get out of the China visit? In tangible terms, probably not much. Despite Mr. Nixon's publication of his peace terms for Vietnam, the chances are that he will get no support in Peking for any such accommodation, but rather a cool lecture on ending the killing and a recommendation that he accept the enemy's terms and get out of Indochina.

On Taiwan, he is almost certain to be asked why he still has several thousand troops in what Chou En-lai considers a province of China, and how would Mr. Nixon like it if China stationed troops in Hawaii or Long Island? On Japan, the Chinese Government's view is that the United States is reviving the militarism of the Japanese people and helping the Japanese establish by economic means the "Co-Prosperity Sphere" they tried to put together by force of arms in the last world war.

So the President is undoubtedly right to minimize the expectations of the American people before he leaves. He may manage to arrange for cultural exchanges between China and the United States, and negotiate some kind of exchange of trade missions or trade agents to explore the possibilities of increasing the commerce between the two countries, but even this is not sure.

In the end, however, the imponderables of these talks may prove to be more important than anything else. We are still far from normalization of U.S.-Chinese diplomatic relations, but the long process of exchanging views and establishing some means of orderly communication will have begun.

Also, it is not clear what part the Sino-Soviet dispute has played in China's willingness to break the long deadlock with Washington. That Peking is concerned over the presence of a million Soviet troops on her northern frontier is obvious from the fact that she is already building deep bunkers and underground shelters in all her main cities, but this is not the sort of dispute Mr. Nixon wants to enter.

After all, he is going on in this year of summits and elections from Peking to Moscow, and it is his purpose, not to take sides in the Sino-Soviet troubles, but to improve Washington's relations with both China and the Soviet Union, and if possible to lessen the tensions between the two Communist giants.

All this, however, will take some doing and some time. The President has been careful to reassure Moscow, Tokyo, London, Paris, Bonn, Seoul and Taipei that he is not going to Peking to make deals at the expense of any of his allies, but merely to reduce tensions wherever he can. And if he can do that, it will be a useful journey, even if he brings back nothing more than a cultural agreement and a little more trust that China and America can talk again about the common problems of the Pacific.

Three Wars, Three Ways

By C. L. SULZBERGER

FOREIGN AFFAIRS

JERUSALEM—Nowadays Asia is the most warlike continent and has replaced Europe as the scene of great power competition to gain influence in the global balance. During recent years there have been successive mini-wars in Yemen, along Arabia's Trucial coast, between the Kurds and Iraqis, among Pathan tribesmen, the Naga hill people and in Burma, where civil conflict is so common as to be the norm.

But the three great areas of contention have been West Asia, where the Israeli-Arab war has had three violent flare-ups and, in between, never really ceased; South Asia, where there have likewise been three major confrontations between Indians and Pakistanis; and Southeast Asia where the Indochina struggle seems a tragically permanent feature of the world's political landscape.

The Chinese civil war and the Korean conflict came and went (despite occasional faint rumors that the latter may revive). But the three battlefields of West, South and Southeast Asia remain disruptive danger points and in each the influence and policies of three major powers—the United States, Soviet Russia and People's China—can be felt.

In all three, American and Soviet policies have been openly hostile to each other, with each supporting client states in local conflicts although conspiring in the end to prevent small wars from becoming big. And in all three, likewise, China has played its own role, opposing both superpowers while switching about between them.

Thus in the Middle East, Russia is now the Arab champion while the United States gives immense support to this little state once described accordingly to his President by an American ambassador: "You know Israel may be a small horse but it's the only horse we are riding that has four sound legs." China is anti-Israel but, rather than competing for influence in the Arab states, it concentrates on trying to influence Arab guerrillas and revolutionary movements by outflanking Russia from the left.

In South Asia the U.S.A. and China recently found themselves virtually cobelligerents when they backed Pakistan in its brief confrontation with Soviet-supported India. This marked a dramatic departure from traditional U.S. policy which, although allied to Pakistan, had sought to build up India as an Asiatic counterpoise to China.

In Southeast Asia the United States increasingly helped South Vietnam and anti-Communist factions in Laos and Cambodia ever since France was extruded from the area eighteen years ago. Russia and China vied for influence in Hanoi but, since Ho Chi Minh's death, Moscow has gained the upper hand.

• There appears to be curious interrelationship between the attitudes of Washington, Moscow and Peking on these Asian crisis spots. In the Middle East, where danger of holocaust remains intense, the superpowers have gone to the brink but in the end signaled each other to draw back. Chinese influence was minimal in the crunch.

In South Asia both China and the United States, working with rare harmony, made bluff maneuvers against India's land and sea frontiers but quietly wilted when Pakistan collapsed. Moscow gained a great triumph over Peking and Washington.

In Southeast Asia, American policy is desperately trying to find a way to settlement without ignoble collapse and Chinese opposition to such efforts seems to have diminished. But the Russian are urging Hanoi to fight on and humiliate the U. S. world image.

In each area of confrontation the external great powers, pursuing their own interests, have not hesitated to shift their stands. The Arabs were amazed to see Russia veto a U.N. proposal to halt fighting and call for Indian troop withdrawals in South Asia when Moscow had backed precisely the same resolution during the latest war with Israel. The United States likewise reversed field on exactly the same issue.

The Chinese used to prod the Vietnamese Communists to fight to the very end and even made hostile military gestures to warn off the United States. Now they are lying relatively low and even have encouraged Prince Sihanouk of Cambodia to denounce Soviet policy while they prepare to receive President Nixon in Peking.

The shifting great power maneuvers around the vortices of Asian trouble have been astonishing. The only constant external force is the U. N.—as a nonforce. Time and again it has been shown in Asia as wholly paralyzed and capable of neither preventing wars nor halting them.

The Course of Military Justice

By TELFORD TAYLOR

As a signatory of the Geneva Convention of 1949, the United States is bound to "search for" and bring to trial all persons who have committed "grave breaches" of the laws of war, and to "enact any legislation necessary to provide effective penal sanctions for persons committing" grave breaches. As the nation which for over a century took the lead in codifying and applying the laws of war, the United States is bound to govern the conduct of its armed forces by the standards that have been applied to the soldiers of Germany, Japan and other nations.

Now that the last of the courts-martial relating to the Mylai killings has concluded, it is time to assess our Government's role and obligations.

Ten enlisted men, one platoon leader and the company commander were charged with criminal responsibility for the Mylai killings. No effort was made to bring to trial any officer at a higher level, or anyone who had left military service prior to public disclosure of the killings. Three of the enlisted men charged were brought to trial; all were acquitted, and thereafter the charges against the others were dropped.

Ably prosecuted, the platoon leader, Lieut. William Calley, was convicted of first-degree murder and sentenced to imprisonment for life, subsequently reduced to 20 years. Strongly defended, the company commander, Capt. Ernest Medina, was acquitted.

Since over a year passed between the Mylai killings and disclosure of the episode, the Army established a high-level board of review, headed by Lieut. Gen. William R. Peers, to inquire into the circumstances of the "cover-up." On the basis of the board's findings, charges of perjury and other derelictions connected with the cover-up were filed against 14 officers, including the divisional commander, a major general.

Thereafter the charges against 13 of the 14 were dismissed without trial. Col. Oran Henderson alone was tried, and acquitted. Captain Medina, who freely admitted that he had concealed the killings, was not charged with the cover-up.

While the several courts-martial were in process, the Peers report was rightly held confidential. The Army has announced that it will not be released, at least until the review of Calley's case is completed. But Pentagon Papers and Anderson papers have now been followed by "Peers papers," and much of the contents of the report have been disclosed in articles by Seymour Hersh in The New Yorker. According to the Hersh account, the Peers report shows that the killings at Mylai were not confined to the men of Calley's platoon, or even of Medina's company, though the Army has never brought charges in connection with these other units, or even acknowledged that they occurred.

Although many persons participated in or were otherwise responsible for the Mylai killings, only Lieutenant Calley has been found guilty. And, although the killings were unlawfully concealed and numerous officers were involved, no one has been found criminally responsible for the cover-up. It is apparent that the Army's procedures for the prevention, detection, and punishment of war crimes have failed abysmally. It is equally apparent that the United States has seriously defaulted on its international obligations under the Geneva Conventions.

Calley's personal guilt is beyond question, but the idea that he alone should bear criminal responsibility is absurd. Certainly no deterrent purpose can be served by punishing only Calley, and so irrational an outcome tends to degrade rather than exalt the judicial process. Under the circumstances, commutation or suspension of Calley's sentence is appropriate, *but only if done for the right reasons*. Any clemency for Calley which implies that what he and the others did at Mylai was "really not so bad" would turn a disgraceful situation into an unspeakable one. The "greatest reason" is to do "the right deed for the wrong reason," T. S. Eliot had Thomas Becket say.

Clemency for Calley should be granted, if at all, on the basis that it is unfitting and unprincipled to punish one man for the crime of many. It should be accompanied by an avowal that the Army's procedures proved inadequate to cope with the problems of the Mylai killings.

Over the years, the United States Army has done as well as most and better than many others in requiring its men to comply with the laws of the war. This generally good record makes it doubly important to perceive the causes of failure in connection with Mylai.

The Government failed to take proper account of the Supreme Court's 1955 decision that ex-servicemen are not answerable to court-martial for accusations of crime committed while in service. That decision should have stimulated legislative action to confer on the Federal courts, or other suitable tribunals, jurisdiction over such offenses. The Government's failure was a plain breach of our obligation, under the Geneva Conventions, "to enact any legislation necessary to provide effective penal sanctions" for war crimes. The consequence of this failure was that those involved in Mylai who had left the service before the disclosures were immune.

Captain Medina did not personally participate in the mass killings at Mylai, and the charge against him in this respect was based on the well-established doctrine of "command responsibility"—the duty, as described in the Army field manual on the law of land warfare, "to take the necessary and reasonable steps to insure compliance with the laws of war" by his troops. The manual is explicit that this duty attaches when the commander "has actual knowledge, or should have knowledge" that his troops are committing or about to commit war crimes. A commander must not, whether deliberately or negligently, fail to acquire information about his troops' actions necessary for his responsibilities.

But the military judge before whom Medina was tried, in his charge to the jury, omitted the "should have" portion of the rule and instructed the jury that they could not find Medina guilty unless he had "actual knowledge." He also charged them not to find Medina guilty unless they were satisfied that unlawful killings of Mylai villagers took place after the time at which he acquired actual knowledge. Since no one was holding a stopwatch on the morning's doings in Mylai, it is hard to see how a conscientious jury could have made any such finding.

It is clear that the charge virtually dictated acquittal, and that it was squarely contrary to the laws of war as set forth in the Army's own field manual. It is likewise clear that Medina's acquittal effectively immunized all those above him in the chain of command, for if the company captain, within earshot of the killings and in radio communication with the guilty unit, could not be found liable, how could colonels and generals overhead in helicopters?

The fiasco with respect to the cover-up was largely due to the independent authority which the military judicial system gives to the commander of the headquarters to which an accused officer is assigned. In 13 of the 14 cases in which the Peers board recommended charges, the headquarters commanders in substance overruled the board and ordered the charges dismissed.

Apart from the failure of the Army's judicial machinery, there has been an even more serious deficiency in the Government's response to the Mylai disclosures. The several courts-martial have done little to inform the public on the broader questions raised by the episode. What were the antecedent circumstances of training and leadership which made Mylai possible? What are the legal and human consequences of Army operational standards and practices in Southeast Asia, such as "body count" reports, "free-fire" and "free-strike" zones, mass removals of civilians from their homes, crop destruction and defoliation?

Now that the criminal process has run its sorry course, a number of other measures are urgently necessary. These should include:

(1) Review of Calley's sentence in the light of the failure to convict anyone else;

(2) Enactment of legislation authorizing appropriate tribunals to try ex-servicemen accused of crimes committed while in service outside the United States;

(3) Publication of the Peers report and the documents and testimony on which it was based;

(4) Creation of a national commission of inquiry, vested with power to compel testimony and grant immunity, in accordance with the recent recommendations of the Association of the Bar of the City of New York. The commission's range of investigation should include at a minimum the military operational directives in force in Southeast Asia, the standards of training and discipline with regard to observance of the laws of war, and the processes of military justice in dealing with war crimes.

Only by treating the end of the courts-martial as the beginning of serious efforts to confront the facts and learn from experience can the failure of the judicial process be redeemed, and the stain of Mylai lightened.

Telford Taylor, chief U.S. prosecutor of Nazi Germany's war criminals at the Nuremberg trials and a professor of law at Columbia, is author of "Nuremberg and Vietnam: An American Tragedy."

Eugene Mihaesco

Breaking Up City Hall: III

How to Decentralize Intelligently and Painlessly

By ALAN K. CAMPBELL

SYRACUSE—Neighborhoods, particularly in large cities, have been rediscovered, not by the people who live in them—they've always known about them—but by political activists and theorists of right and left. A growing body of nonideological scholars and citizens also are seeking ways to increase citizens' control over their own lives and over the quality and quantity of local services—especially services which touch people who live in the least affluent areas of our great cities.

The neighborhood or local community control movement departs sharply from an evolutionary pattern of change over the last half century. This pattern expanded local jurisdictions, moved intrajurisdictional power from political parties and legislatures to chief executives, and gradually increased the national Government's power and influence.

The advantages claimed for decentralization and community control are not unlike the supposed benefits of the earlier centralization: more responsive, efficient government; equity in the provision of government services; and greater concern for Americans whom government had bypassed, mistreated, discriminated against, or plain forgotten. Analyses of localism and states' rights over the last half-century have suggested that the potential benefits of these decentralized grass-roots governments were vitiated by excessive conservatism in state and local government.

Despite these social policy gains from greater centralization, the decentralizers point to quite different results of the increasing centralization of American governmental institutions. Professionalism, credentialism, separation of policymaking from administration, and nonpartisanism have all been effectively used, they claim, to reduce the average citizens' influence on government.

Despite legitimate criticisms of our system, many reformers seem to argue that more of the same, not less, will solve our problems. They advocate metropolitan or regional government to replace local government, thus continuing past centralizing tendencies.

The metropolitanists maintain that community control and local autonomy would exacerbate present disparities. For example, a ghetto student who now receives $100-$200 less than his suburban counterpart in educational support, would, under community control, face a gap of several more hundred dollars if the local community's tax base became the basic source of educational funds.

The evident legitimacy of arguments for both centralization and decentralization underscores our need for a system which recognizes the validity of each. The present system denies both, particularly as they apply to the nation's largest urban areas.

Metropolitan government without a second-tier, community level, deserves the criticism heaped upon it by advocates of community control. Critics of metro offer New York City as proof of the failure of this governmental form.

New York metro is in trouble because, first, it has ceased being metropolitan. Its creation also destroyed smaller, well-knit communities within the boroughs. Complete restructuring of the New York system on a two-tier model would provide a system which, region-wide, would recognize the reality of fiscal disparities and technological imperatives alike. Certain services would be regionalized, while, simultaneously, communities with real power would be recreated within the city. Such a system could overcome functional and jurisdictional fragmentation, and open the entire region's tax base as a resource to meet needs that are concentrated in the region's disadvantaged areas. At the same time, a revived sense of local community identity and power could flourish without becoming the nostalgia for a romanticized small-town past which occasionally afflicts radical decentralizers.

Gathered within city boundaries are Gulliverian social problems that must be fought from a Lilliputian tax-base—a base at best staying level, at worst declining absolutely. A system embracing the entire metropolitan area, underpinned by community governments, will offer much greater potential political power to minority communities than our present system does. New coalitions across the region will become possible. Everyone in the region will share access to a growing tax base. The possibility overcoming the present mismatch of resources to needs—a mismatch between city and suburbia as well as between high and low income suburbs will then be possible.

Alan K. Campbell is dean, Maxwell Graduate School, Syracuse University.

Contents

A Game of Cosmic Roulette
An Interview with Jacques Monod

The following is an interview with Jacques Monod, 1965 Nobel Prize winner in biology and author of "Chance and Necessity."

Q. You write that man was the product of pure chance. How do you come to that conclusion?

A. Well, it's relatively simple in principle, unless we accept the pure creationist view of the orgins of the universe. Unless we do that, we have to find some form of natural interpretation.

I think the basic attitude of science, as defined after Galileo, is what I call the postulated objectivity. It's a negative postulate. It says that no interpretation of whatever happens in terms of final causes is acceptable. Now that's a pure postulate because clearly you can't prove that this is right.

If you start with this, then you are faced with the advanced paradox that within the cosmos there is no intention. There is no project. There comes about the biosphere full of systems which behave as if they had a project. This is the core problem in biology—how do we account for the fact that purposeful systems could have grown out of a universe devoid of purpose?

The understanding of how this could have happened is that the whole business started with certain microscopic structures which had the unique capacity of reproducing not only their structure, but also any accident which had happened within that structure. And that's the unique property of human beings.

Evolution by itself is not a privilege of human beings.

Any microscopic structure undergoes evolution, changes with time, because of small mutations which occur in the structure, and therefore tend to modify it. In fact, as a general rule, they tend to bring more and more disorder into that structure. With this, you immediately set up a huge roulette which is going to throw out numbers at a fantastic rate, and from time to time a good number is going to come out.

Q. What is a good number?

A. A good number is one which gives even better opportunities for this invariant self-producing structure to reproduce even faster, or better, or under new conditions.

We know the nature of those accidents within the structure. We know these accidents to be microscopic.

We can write chemical formulae corresponding to a mutation in the genetic code and we therefore know, as well as one can know anything in science, that there is no source of novelty in the biosphere other than the microscopic accidents. We also know that these microscopic accidents cannot and will probably never be treated in any way other than as accidents—as chance events: for the very simple but at the same time profound reason that they are microscopic accidents.

Now if we come to man, we must accept the fact that within the biosphere the emergence of man is a unique event. I'm not saying that is dependent on a single mutation. It must have involved a great many mutations. Interestingly, we don't know how many.

Maybe we will some day. But there's no question that each of these accidents was a chance event. And what has created man is a combination of chance events, whose probability was even, of course, much lower than any of the individual chance events.

So I don't think any serious biologist today would dispute this statement: that before the appearance of man, had there been a first-rate scientific brain lurking around, this first-rate brain could not possibly have predicted this event.

There's one point which I have made in the book, perhaps not strongly enough, which I find extremely significant. While man, from a purely biological, physiological, morphological point of view, has nothing unique, and while his general biochemistry and physiology are exactly the same as mammals, he is absolutely unique in one respect, namely language. And that language would be, of course, the vehicle that opens up the possibility of culture.

The mere fact that this event occurred only once by itself indicates that it was not written somewhere in the evolution of the biosphere that language should appear.

Q. If I believe this thesis . . .

A. You cannot *not* believe it! There's no alternative. Either accepting this thesis, or taking a mythical or religious attitude, which of course cannot be disallowed. It is, of course, far simpler to accept a universe with an intention and with someone to guide its evolution.

Q. You talk about the fact that Western man, especially, has a need for explaining his existence.

A. This is very important because it is precisely that need that causes our ethical attitudes.

If I psychoanalyze myself, I'm a mixture of existentialism and intellectual Puritanism. I don't see any other possibility except once more—some sort of religious belief.

Q. Do we have some type of very deep psychological need to think that we're here for a reason? Maybe a certain insecurity of Western man that he can't accept that he's here truly by chance. He's developed philosophies and religions and myths for so many years . . .

A. All of which gave him a place in the universe. It's something exceedingly difficult to accept.

Q. Does Jean-Paul Sartre agree with you?

A. I think Jean-Paul Sartre should agree with me on the ethical conclusions; because essentially they are what we define as an existentialist attitude.

Q. How does this affect a poet, or a novelist? Much of Western literary tradition had been an attempt to explain man's relation to the universe. Do you think that anyone writing literature today has to come to grips now with what you say in "Chance and Necessity"?

A. I definitely think so. But I didn't invent this, you see. All this has been said before. The only originality is the logical thread which runs through the book.

If we accept the scientific attitude, if we accept the postulated objectivity, if we say that we are not going to recognize as knowledge any statement which is not based on the postulated objectivity, then we are forced into these conclusions—there's absolutely no way of getting out of it. It's literally a prison that we have built for ourselves.

Q. The Western world seems to have suffered a nervous breakdown. People say society doesn't work. Life is becoming more and more difficult to understand and enjoy. Do you think you provide an answer to what people seem to be groping for?

A. I would say that I attempt to delineate the types of answers or the type of answer that would be logically acceptable. Now to say that it would be logically acceptable does not imply that it will be psychologically acceptable.

It seems to me that one of the causes, not the only one but, perhaps, the most profound, is the one that attacks the soul. We live in societies that have developed on the basis of strong and widely accepted systems of value which are a more or less harmonious blend of the ideas of the philosophers of the Enlightenment, particularly Rousseau. Man is good and there is something called the natural rights of man which have to be sustained. It's an absolute law; since these are natural rights, we are therefore bound to defend them. Of course, if you analyze this idea of natural rights of man, it doesn't stand for a minute. There's no such thing as the natural rights of man.

In what way are they natural? Nobody could answer that.

We cannot believe in natural rights of man, nor can we believe in the religious basis of the Christian value system. Mind you, I'm not attacking the Christian value system. What I'm attacking are the mythological or metaphysical grounds upon which these values were purported to stand.

Q. This seems to be, I think, the greatest misunderstanding, because I have the impression that we have to wipe the slate clean and start all over again. Is everything that we've been believing for 2,000 years bunk? If so, then the question arises: Are you trying to create a sterile society?

A. Of course not. What I'm saying is that we have values that we operate by, and certainly a scrutiny of these values individually must be gone through, but this is not to mean that we're going to give them all up—it's ridiculous—values of love, of creativity, of respect for freedom and dignity in man, and so on, are all things that we certainly want to keep if we can.

But if we pretend to base these values on philosophical or religious systems that cannot stand any more, then they are in danger, and in fact the only way of preserving them is to find some other foundation.

Once you have a system—and that is certainly what the average Marxist creed is—which is all-embracing, and where the history of societies is linked up with the history of evolution in the biosphere, which in turn is linked up with the history of the cosmos, then there is nothing that you could not justify on that basis, absolutely nothing.

Any total system which pretends to understand the real meaning of our lives and of humanity has this inherent danger. One has to distinguish between the operational value system that a society works by, which is more or less reflected in its constitution, its laws, and so on, and the logical and philosophical justification of this complete system. We have no acceptable justification today. And my interpretation of the *mal de l'âme* is just that.

Q. If Charles de Gaulle were alive today, how do you think he'd react to your thesis?

A. I would think that the conclusions would have been completely unacceptable to him. He was a man of the 17th century. His whole political action was based on mythological concepts of nations and a profound lack of respect for man—individual man. Institutions, for him, had to be saved. Institutions and nationry. And man was just a passing nothing at the service of these institutions.

Who Speaks for Ethnic America?

By Barbara Mikulski

The Ethnic American is forgotten and forlorn. He is infuriated at being used and abused by the media, government and business. Pejorative epithets such as "pigs" and "racists" or slick, patronizing labels like the "silent majority" or "hard hats" are graphic examples of the lack of respect, understanding and appreciation of him and his way of life.

The Ethnic Americans are 40 million working class Americans who live primarily in 58 major industrial cities like Baltimore and Chicago. Our roots are in Central and Southern Europe. We have been in this country for one, two or three generations. We have made a maximum contribution to the U.S.A., yet received minimal recognition.

The ethnics came to America from the turn of the century through the twenties, until we were restricted by prejudicial immigration quotas—65,000 Anglo-Saxons to 300 Greeks. We came looking for political freedom and economic opportunity. Many fled from countries where there had been political, religious and cultural oppression for 1,000 years.

It was this working class which built the Great Cities—constructed the skyscrapers, operated the railroads, worked on the docks, factories, steel mills and in the mines. Though our labor was in demand, we were not accepted. Our names, language, food and cultural customs were the subject of ridicule. We were discriminated against by banks, institutions of higher learning and other organizations controlled by the Yankee Patricians. There were no protective mechanisms for safety, wages and tenure. We called ourselves Americans. We were called "wop," "polack" and "hunky."

For our own protection, we formed our own institutions and organizations and clung together in our new neighborhoods. We created communities like "Little Italy" and "Polish Hill." The ethnic parish church and the fraternal organizations like the Polish Womens' Alliance and the Sons of Italy became the focal points of our culture.

These neighborhoods were genuine "urban villages." Warmth, charm and zesty communal spirit were their characteristics. People knew each other. This was true not only of relatives and friends but of the grocer, politician and priest. The people were proud, industrious and ambitious. All they wanted was a chance to "make it" in America.

Here we are in the 1970's, earning from $5,000 to $10,000 per year. We are "near poor" economically. No one listens to our problems. The President's staff responds to our problems by patronizingly patting us on the head and putting pictures of construction workers on postage stamps. The media stereotype us as gangsters or dumb clods in dirty sweat-shirts. The status of manual labor has been denigrated to the point where men are often embarrassed to say they are plumbers or tugboat operators. This robs men of the pride in their work and themselves.

The Ethnic American is losing ground economically. He is the victim of both inflation and anti-inflation measures. Though wages have increased by 20 per cent since the mid-sixties, true purchasing power has remained the same. He is hurt by layoffs due to cutbacks in production and construction. Tight money policies strangle him with high interest rates for installment buying and mortgages. He is the man who at 40 is told by the factory bosses that he is too old to be promoted. The old job is often threatened by automation. At the same time, his expenses are at their peak. He is paying on his home and car, probably trying to put at least one child through college.

In pursuing his dream of home ownership, he finds that it becomes a millstone rather than a milestone in his life. Since FHA loans are primarily restricted to "new" housing, he cannot buy a house in the old neighborhood. He has no silk-stocking lawyers or fancy lobbyists getting him tax breaks.

He believes in the espoused norms of American manhood like "a son should take care of his mother" and "a father should give his children every opportunity." Yet he is torn between putting out $60 a month for his mother's arthritis medication or paying for his daughter's college tuition.

When the ethnic worker looks for some modest help, he is told that his income is too high. He's "too rich" to get help when his dad goes into a nursing home. Colleges make practically no effort to provide scholarships to kids named Colstiani, Slukowski or Klima.

The one place where he felt the master of his fate and had status was in his own neighborhood. Now even that security is being threatened. He wants new schools for his children and recreation facilities for the entire family—not just the token wading pool for pre-schoolers or the occasional dance for teen-agers. He wants his street fixed and his garbage collected. He finds that the only things being planned for his area are housing projects, expressways and fertilizer factories. When he goes to City Hall to make his problems known, he is either put off, put down or put out.

Liberals scapegoat us as racists. Yet there was no racial prejudice in our hearts when we came. There were very few black people in Poland or Lithuania. The élitists who now smugly call us racists are the ones who taught us the meaning of the word: their bigotry extended to those of a different class or national origin.

Government is further polarizing people by the creation of myths that black needs are being met. Thus the ethnic worker is fooled into thinking that the blacks are getting everything.

Old prejudices and new fears are ignited. The two groups end up fighting each other for the same jobs and competing so that the new schools and recreation centers will be built in their respective communities. What results is angry confrontation for tokens, when there should be an alliance for a whole new Agenda for America. This Agenda would be created if black and white organized separately in their own communities for their own needs and came together to form an alliance based on mutual issues, interdependence and respect. This alliance would develop new strategies for community organization and political restructuring. From this, the new Agenda for America would be generated. It could include such items as "new towns in town," innovative concepts of work and creative structures for community control.

What is necessary is to get rid of the guilt of phony liberals, control by economic élitists and manipulation by selfish politicians. Then, let us get on with creating the democratic and pluralistic society that we say we are.

Barbara Mikulski is a Baltimore city council woman.

'Someday Us Poor Is Going to Overrule'

By Shirley Dalton

DELLSLOW, W. Va.—It's always been trouble for us. We've fought from day to day, fought worrying about where's the next meal coming from.

I'm not drawing welfare now, thank God no. But, my God! My husband is working hauling limestone. Still, he's not getting to work every day. People is in better shape on welfare than they are taking these jobs Nixon put in here.

On the welfare, I drew $182 a month. And I got food stamps for $56 out of that. And my doctor bills was being paid, and my hospital and medicine I need on account of I'm an epileptic. My pills I gotta have the rest of my life.

Okay. On welfare I didn't have to worry about that. But, now, since Darris has got a job and not making but 40 cents over standard pay, I been cut off. And my food stamps got raised and they took my medical card away. So what am I supposed to do?

When my kids get sick, I don't take them to a hospital. I can't. I've been there and I know what the place is. They don't want you if you've not got the money to lay right there in their hands. They turn you away.

I took my daughter over there to the hospital. She got hurt at school. They had to call a special doctor down to the hospital. Her ligaments in her leg was all pulled. Her leg completely twisted. And he came over there and he jerked on that leg. She give out a scream. Well, he slammed her leg down and he said to me, "You take her home. She's a bawl baby and I ain't gonna work on her." And he didn't.

There's three rooms in this house. With nine of us living here it's not that peaceful. We lived in two rooms till last summer. My kids has to sleep on the floor right there in front of the coal fire. It's not that safe with all that bedding so close up to the fire. People can look and they can say, "You don't try to do nothing." But how are you suppose to?

I might be poor, I might not have much, but I can give a dollar to this boy up here who's dying of a kidney disease.

There was one time when my husband went to work for the O.E.O. He worked on the roads with some other men. Well, they never did get their paychecks. They couldn't afford to even buy the gas to drive to work. Well, the O.E.O. man told all the workers one day, "If you all don't show up for work tomorrow, you're fired." But the men couldn't get there. And every one of them got fired. All of them.

We went one month without no help of any kind. We had no coal. We had nothing. No gas nor nothing to cook with. We didn't have nothing to eat anyhow. I went into Morgantown and I asked the welfare for coal. They wouldn't give it to me. They gave me a $7 food stamp for the nine of us. Now, that's what we lived off for one month. I had one loaf of bread to divide up between us. We chopped wood. And when it snowed back up in there, I couldn't get out for nothing. The worst part was having to see the kids go hungry. Oh, no, and don't they say people in this country don't starve. They ain't never seen the day come.

Now, I have a boy that's 14. And he don't want to go to school. He's afraid. He's been knocked, hit in the head, his clothes were torn off him, and the cook at the schoolhouse knocked his legs out from under him, him with his tray—put a knot on his head.

Now, a boy's a boy, I don't care who they are. They're gonna be bad. That don't mean the teacher's gotta beat him. Now. They get a lunch ticket. The teacher told my boy if he loses his lunch ticket once more, he gets no more. Now, I can't afford to pay for their lunches. For four days he went without lunch and I never knew it. He'd lost his ticket and was afraid to ask for it. And, he's got pride.

I don't want my kids to be ashamed. When they got to live on welfare they gotta live on it. But they ought not to be ashamed over it. I'd rather see them eating than to see them have false pride.

I can see it in the stores. People is ashamed they got food stamps. Their faces is as red as a beet. But I can't see being ashamed. Because before I'm going to let my kids go hungry I'm gonna fight.

Anyway, I'm proud to be poor. I'm glad I hain't got anything anybody else has got. These rich people that's got all the money, they don't know what it is to have got a hurt. But when the hurt hurts them, nobody will look at them and say, "You helped me when I was out. Now it's my turn to help you." Nobody will be there.

Darris is up there now, driving a truck off the mountain. Why, if that truck turned over, something fell on him, my God, he could be killed just the same as any miner. When the miners is making $40 and $50 a day, why us people, our food prices goes up too. And we're living on $12, $13 a day.

We can't afford to buy coal now and winter coming on. And what am I going to do next year?

My epilepsy pills is about run out now. I don't know how I'm gonna get some more. Darris drawed $72 this last paycheck. We had 50 cents left after we paid our bills.

The time will come. Someday us poor is going to overrule. We're gonna do it, by the help of God we're gonna do it. I believe it. I honest to God do, I believe it. The poor is going to overrule. I've got faith in that.

This is adapted from "Hillbilly Women," edited by Kathy Kahn.

As the Days Dwindle Down

By Lyndon B. Johnson

TEMPLE, Tex.—With the coming of September each year, we are reminded as the song says, that the days are dwindling down to a precious few. By the calendar, we know that soon the green leaves of summer will begin to brown; the chill winds of winter will begin to blow; and—before we are ready for the end to come—the year will be gone.

If we permit our thoughts to dwell upon this perspective, these days can become a melancholy season.

As it is with the calendar, so it sometimes seems to be with our country and its system. For there are those among us who would have us believe that America has come to its own September. That our days are dwindling down to a precious few. That the green leaves of our best season are turning brown and will soon be falling to the ground. That before long we will feel the first chill wind of a long American winter—and that our nation's stand as mankind's "last best hope" will be done.

For those who preach this prophecy—and for those who believe it—this period of our affairs can only be a melancholy season. But it is to that mood—and to the perceptions which foster it—that I want to address my remarks today.

Over the course of a long, full and gratifying life, I have seen many Septembers and have known many autumns. In public service—and in private life—I have experienced a full measure of unwelcome winters. Yet melancholy is not a mood which I have ever allowed to weigh for long upon my spirits.

I live—as I have always worked—by the faith that with each passing day, we are always approaching nearer to the beginning of a new springtime. It is by that perspective I see our country now.

If I believe anything of this land—if I know anything of its people and their character—I believe and I know that we have not come to and are not approaching America's September.

On the contrary, it is my conviction—a conviction which deepens every day—that this land and its people are quickening with the new life and new potential of what will become the springtime of a new America.

I do not say this merely to offer reassurance in anxious times. Far from it, I intend what I say to be taken as a challenge—a challenge to every citizen of every age.

No nation can be more than the visions of its people. Americans cannot be more than we believe ourselves capable of becoming. Thus we are directly challenged to choose between two very different perceptions of what we are and what we can make of America itself.

On the one hand, we can choose to guide our course by the light of the bright perceptions—of America the beautiful, America the just, America the land of the free and the home of the brave.

Or, on the other hand, we can choose to move toward the shadows of what some have called "the dark perception" of America the unclean, America the unjust, America the unworthy.

For myself—as, I am sure, for many of you—there is no real choice. I want to open the soul of America to the warm sunlight of faith in itself, faith in the principles and precepts of its birth, faith in the promise and potential of its resources and skills and people. Yet I know that, in these times, this is not easy.

For too long, we have permitted the dark perception to pervade our midst. Day after day, month after month, the portrayal of America as unclean, unjust and unworthy has been ground into the consciousness of our people.

We no longer see the blooming flowers for we are searching for the litter. We no longer celebrate the many fresh triumphs of justice for we are lingering over the residue of yesterday's shortcomings. We no longer measure the miles we have come toward a more humane, civil and peaceful world for we are too busy calibrating the remaining inches of times we are trying to escape and leave behind.

This is our clear and present challenge.

When we permit these dark perceptions to dominate us, we are allowing our future to be shaped by visions that are small and mean and diminishing to our potential. We are, in simple terms, dooming those who come after us to know what could only be a second-rate America.

This is a future which I am unwilling to accept.

I have devoted my time on this earth to working toward the day when there would be no second-class citizenship in America, no second-quality opportunity, no second-hand justice at home, no second-place status in the world for our ideals and benefits.

I do not intend now that second-rate visions shall set our course toward settling for a second-rate America. That is why I speak as I do now.

All through the pages of history we read the heart-rending stories of those who set out in quest of great goals and discoveries, yet when they were almost to the edge of success, they hesitated—not knowing or understanding how near they were to their aims. Out of that moment of hesitation, all too often they lost forever their opportunity to succeed.

In many respects, that seems to me to be a pattern we ourselves are in danger of repeating.

Over all the years of our nation's existence, we have been setting goals for ourselves and striving tirelessly to reach them. Those goals have been both the slogans and the substance of national affairs for generation after generation.

Full employment. Decent wages. Adequate housing. Education for everyone. Opportunity for all. Good health, good medical care, good hospitals for even the least among us. Above all, equal justice under the law for all our fellow men. America's goals have been simple and basic.

They have permeated and motivated all our institutions—churches and schools, professions and labor unions and corporations and foundations—as well as our government at every level.

All our American resources and strengths—private and public—have been committed to the effort and we have come very close to success.

Nowhere—over all the globe—have any people, under any other system, come nearer to fulfillment of such aspirations than we have under our system.

Yet, at the very moment we were near to realization, we have allowed our effort to go slack, our momentum to slow and we have entered a season of hesitation.

Why?

Basically, I believe, it is because we have not understood—and still do not fully comprehend—where we are or what we are about.

Whatever may be your own perception of where we are and where we may be heading, let me say for myself that I see little today suggesting that our system is failing—but I see all too much which convincingly argues that by our doubts and hesitation we may be failing the promise and potential of our system.

We are not living in times of collapse. The old is not coming down. Rather, the troubling and torment these days stem from the new trying to rise into place.

With our nation's past efforts, with our long and faithfully kept commitments, with our infinite successes in so many fields, we have brought into being the materials, as it were, with which to construct a new America.

Faced with the task of such great dimensions, we have no time for melancholy. We have no cause for moroseness. We have work to be done—the greatest work any generation of Americans has ever faced. Believing that, I say—let's be on with our labors.

The essentials of a new America—a better America—are all on hand and within our reach. It is our destiny—and I believe, our duty—to take up our appointed positions and commence the labors that will change what needs change among us.

Our real challenge lies not in suppressing change but utilizing it to vitalize and energize our society. Change is not our enemy. On the contrary, this society has no deadlier danger than refusal to change.

This is what I believe our young Americans are trying—and have been trying—to communicate to us. With their fine young minds, fresh new learning and clear new vision, they are seeing many segments of our society as it needs to be seen and understood.

The most frightening thing that could happen to us today would be for us to close our eyes to new ideas, and to close our ears to those—particularly the young, in whom we have invested so much hope and effort through the years of our existence—who are trying to tell us how they would go about perfecting the visions of America.

It is just such spirit that we honor on this occasion. It is by restoring that spirit to our lives and our nation's life that we can honor our own trust as Americans.

This article was adapted from a 1972 address by President Johnson at the Scott and White Clinic in Temple, Tex.

'Some of Us Went Hungry'

By a Migrant Worker

LA BELLE, Fla.—I am writing in hopes that in some way The Times may be able to help many people that really need and deserve help from someone, for we are really the forgotten people.

I guess God meant for me to write: We can't get any help from the press here for they depend on the big-money people for their business and if they tried to help the poor old hungry migrant farm worker it wouldn't be good for business.

Hundreds of us that are out of work have tried every way we know to get help. We've met with the commissioners and anyone else that would meet with us, but no luck, farmers want to keep us hungry and broke so we will work for almost anything. Now we have had people sent to investigate but I can truthfully say they never tried in any way to find out the truth. This county and the others around here are small so we don't have any rights but I feel like it's our hard work that puts the fruit and vegetables on everyone's table so maybe somewhere there is people that will try to help. Hundreds of us have been without work since May except for a few day's work and we crawl on our hands and knees for nine hours a day in the hot sun for $12. We might get a day now and then, but all summer, some of us went hungry and several families thrown on the street because they couldn't pay rent.

Hundreds of hungry people standing in line for a meal and a few groceries, and the "Omica"—Organized Migrants In Community Action—got out and went around to stores to beg food to feed these people.

Oh, they have food stamps here but they are so high we can't afford them, for we don't have work so no money.

Here is an example of how the food stamp program is: If you have $14 you can get $28 in food stamps that have to do a month and we have no money for other bills.

I'm about to lose my trailer and have my electricity turned off because I can't pay the bills. This is the rainy season here so my husband doesn't get much work either. Another thing, there are lots of people that need medical attention but we only have a clinic that we can go to once a week, and then there is nothing done except a few pills.

There was one case here where an old colored man was dying. He was taken to one of our county commissioners to get a slip to send him to a doctor. He was refused a doctor, for the commissioner said he would take the matter up at the next meeting, but the old man was dying and couldn't wait, so the lady that had him in the car took him to the police station and he was carried to the hospital. This can be proved by several people.

Now if any of us old migrants gets bad sick, we must hunt up one of our commissioners to get his approval to go to a doctor and you might as well forget it, for the county don't want to pay and to them we are just dirty old farm workers and not human. They use us when they need their work done, any other time they want us to get out of town and get lost until the tomatoes and other stuff is ready to pick. Most of us are good, honest hardworking people that try to work and pay our bills, we have the hardest, dirtiest job in the world, for most of the time we have to crawl all day for almost nothing.

You would think the Government with all the millions of dollars they send to other countries and shoot to the moon, they could spare a little to help us. We are not asking for a handout but just some program that will let us work and earn our own living, for there are a great many people that are still hungry. No work, and when the little work does come we can't start to make enough to pay up our bills for the season only lasts a few weeks and $12 a day isn't very much. Now all of this in this letter can be proved. I can set up a meeting with hundreds of people that are without jobs, anyone can talk to the people and can find out the truth. It's funny, people come around when it's almost election.

I would like to talk to Mr. Nixon or some of his poverty people; they don't know half of it. I don't know what you can do except maybe write a piece in your paper about us and maybe some one will read it that can help us.

I'm giving you my true name and address, but please don't use it for it would be hard for me to get work if the farmers knew we complained but I am writing for all of us farm workers that need help.

On the Occasion of a Death in Boston

By Francis Sweeney

CHESTNUT HILL, Mass.—After the doctor had left, the medication was stopped and for the first time in more days than she could remember her mind was clear. But her body, all weakness and random pain, was something alien to her, a stick figure under the bedspread and the sheet.

She gathered her memories together and in her mind felt almost well again. She remembered the sun-filled days on the North Shore, and Grandfather arriving each evening from Boston. Potter would meet the train at the Prides Crossing station, but Grandfather would take the reins himself and drive at a smart trot the leafy mile to the great house on the shore.

Strange that her memories were of Grandfather, and hardly at all of Father, who with the best will in the world had wasted the fortune and sold off the house at Prides and the town house on Beacon Street. Shamed by sudden poverty, she had taken an office job made for her by Grandfather's friends, and had toiled out a dim life on the edge of the world of her childhood. She lived on Beacon Street, but in a rooming house, where her raffish fellow tenants gave her willing respect and told their friends, quite accurately, that she was a Mayflower descendant.

She stirred in the bed, and tried to turn on her right side. The nurse's aide who came and went helped her to straighten out comfortably, and held a glass of water to her lips.

"I am going to die," she said, and the nurse's aide said, "What gave you that idea? What would you go and die for? Put that out of your mind."

"Am I dirty?" she asked, and the nurse's aide lifted the sheet and said, "Don't you worry about that. I'll fix you up in a jiffy, dear."

And she quickly washed her, and rolled her to one side of the bed and then the other as she changed the sheets. She put a fresh johnnie on her. "Try to think of pleasant things," she said.

Alone again, the old lady tried to find herself in the universe. Pleasant things. She named off the battle roll of her ancestors. There were gravestones with her family name on them at Burial Hill in Plymouth. There were sergeants and cornets in the Revolution, and an ancestor had been breveted colonel after the debacle of Fredericksburg.

"Dirty and dying," she said aloud, and repeated it like a child's nonsense verse. "Dirty and dying, dirty and dying."

The nurse's aide came in again and said, "You must try to sleep, dear."

"I am going to die," the old lady said.

"Nonsense," the nurse's aide said. "Now, haven't you told me that before?"

She was an attractive girl, slight but strong, with woven ropes of blond hair gathered under her white cap. She resembled the upstairs maid at Prides who had lulled a child to sleep, half-humming, half-singing. Often when the child had dropped off to sleep, Grandfather would come up, smelling of port and cigars, and wake her to give him a goodnight kiss.

Pleasant things. All she could remember was lists. An old cotillion card with its list of dances: polka, waltz, schottische, Portland fancy. The wooden plaques Grandfather had nailed up in the garage, each bearing the name of an automobile he had owned: Stevens-Duryea, Mercer, Duesenberg, Marmon, Buick, Packard. The panel wagon from Pierce's rattling up to the kitchen door on Saturday afternoons, with cook standing in the white-tiled kitchen as Pierce's boy piled the groceries on the table.

Now, starting from her yellowed soles the cold was rising up her legs. It was like going into the surf in the early morning at Prides, when the water numbed her as she walked in deeper and struck out with firm strokes. Then the cold, intimate touch of the sea was all over her body.

At last she knew that the rubric of death summoned her. She tried to remember the prayers Reverend Tolliver had given out as they knelt with bowed heads in the upholstered pew, a moment before Grandfather in his white linen suit had walked to the winged lectern to read something incomprehensible from St. Paul.

She remembered the Lord's Prayer, and then as the cold shook her she cried out to the Lord approaching her through the mist, walking on the water. "Well, Lord Jesus, I guess if You want me You'll have to take me as I am."

In the sleepy morning the nurse's aide came up to the lamp-lit desk where the day nurse was reading charts. The day nurse was a solid woman of forty, with thin yellow hair under a cap that rode on her head like a gauze cupcake.

"The poor thing is gone," the nurse's aide said. "We didn't expect her to last the night."

"When did that happen?" the day nurse said.

"Just now, I guess."

The day nurse picked up a stethoscope from the desk and went down the corridor for a few minutes, and then returned. She selected a steel-covered chart from the rack and wrote something in it.

"Shall I wash her up?" the nurse's aide said.

"Don't touch her," the day nurse said. "Don't touch anything until the doctor comes and pronounces her."

"She has a nephew who visited her some weeks ago. He wanted to be notified when she took a turn for the worse," the nurse's aide said.

"Oh, he was notified," the day nurse said.

"Too bad he didn't get here before she died," the nurse's aide said.

"I don't think that will bother him much," the day nurse said.

Father Francis Sweeney teaches English at Boston College.

'Welcome to Santa Fe'

By Robert Mayer

SANTA FE, N. M.—The Indians are sitting in front of the Palace of Governors. Most of them are old, their hair graying, their mouths toothless except for one or two stumps, their copper faces rutted with lifelines. The men wear bandannas around their foreheads, the women wrap themselves in bright-colored shawls, which contrast with their bloated bellies. On the pavement in front of them are blankets spread with rings and necklaces of turquoise and silver; jewelry made at the nearby pueblos, to be sold to passing tourists.

"Welcome to Santa Fe, ladies and gentlemen, the heart of the historic Southwest—where three cultures live in mutual harmony."

A pretty, dark-haired white girl approaches one of the Indian men. "I am a painter," she says. "Would you be willing to pose for me? I pay two dollars an hour."

"I don't do that."

"How about three dollars an hour?"

"I don't do that!"

Bury my . . .

The white girl, red-faced, walks away.

Bury my blush . . .

The Indian remains seated on his milk crate, glaring.

Bury my blush . . . at wounded pride.

In the Plaza across the street is a civic monument, with an inscription carved in stone: "To the heroes who have fallen in the various battles with savage Indians . . . "

An old Chicano man stops a younger Anglo on the street. "I'm looking for a job," he says. "I do gardening, carpentry, I clean out yards. Do you know anybody who has a job?"

"I'm afraid I don't."

"Listen, can you help me out? I haven't eaten in three days."

The Anglo gives the Chicano a quarter. "God bless you," the Chicano says.

Shots ring out in the darkness of an Albuquerque night. Eight hours later the police reveal the results: the bullet-riddled bodies of two young Chicanos. Militants. Brown Berets.

Bury . . .

They were shot while trying to steal dynamite caps at a construction site, the police say. Curious timing. They were supposed to go on television next morning, these dead men, and present evidence of police brutality toward Chicanos. And there are questions: Why did the police wait eight hours before reporting the shootings? Why was no getaway car found at the site? Where is the gun one of the Chicanos allegedly had?

Bury Brown Berets . . .

The district attorney calls the police action "justifiable homicide." The bleeding hearts demand an investigation. A grand jury is convened, and hears evidence—as presented by the district attorney. "Justifiable homicide," the grand jury echoes.

And what of all those questions?

Bury Brown Berets in Albuquerque.

Half a block from the Plaza is the office of Colonias de Santa Fe. Pretty name. Euphonious Colonias.

Colonias is a development corporation. It is planning to build a high-class suburb on the outskirts of Santa Fe. On land leased from an Indian reservation, so it is not subject to local taxes, or local laws. In the face of the mountains that the Spanish named Sangre de Cristos. Blood of Christ.

Bury my . . .

Listen to the poetry of Colonias. It is the poetry of the brochure: "A prestige, master-planned resort suburb . . . Here, people with *joie de vivre* gather to enjoy the splendor of living . . . There is a harmony of manmade beauty . . . Homesites are varied—from estate-size sites to patio homes to garden compound clusters. Recreation—golfing, skiing, tennis, horseback riding, swimming—is bountiful . . . "

Bury my conscience . . .

Never mind the shortage of water, the historic nature of the city, the rugged beauty of the plains. Build. Sell. Sell. Build. Give us your mortgages, your laden bankbooks, for perfect copies of your gleaming suburbs. "Golfing will be at its greatest at Colonias Santa Fe, with a championship 18-hole course designed by the world-famous golf architect Robert Trent Jones."

Bury my . . .

"Oh Beautiful . . . "

Bury my conscience . . .

"God shed His grace . . . "

Bury my restless conscience . . .

on the thirteenth tee.

Robert Mayer is a former New York columnist now living in New Mexico where he is writing a novel.

The Winter of Man

By Loren Eiseley

PHILADELPHIA—
"We fear," remarked an Eskimo shaman responding to a religious question from the explorer Knud Rasmussen some fifty years ago. "We fear the cold and the things we do not understand. But most of all we fear the doings of the heedless ones among ourselves."

Students of the earth's climate have observed that man, in spite of the disappearance of the great continental ice fields, still lives on the steep edge of winter or early spring. The pulsations of these great ice deserts, thousands of feet thick and capable of overflowing mountains and valleys, have characterized the nature of the world since man, in his thinking and speaking phase, arose. The ice which has left the marks of its passing upon the landscape of the Northern Hemisphere has also accounted, in its long, slow advances and retreats, for movements, migrations and extinctions throughout the plant and animal kingdoms.

Though man is originally tropical in his origins, the ice has played a great role in his unwritten history. At times it has constricted his movements, affecting the genetic selection that has created him. Again, ice has established conditions in which man has had to exert all his ingenuity in order to survive. By contrast, there have been other times when the ice has withdrawn farther than today and then, like a kind of sleepy dragon, has crept forth to harry man once more. For something like a million years this strange and alternating contest has continued between man and the ice.

When the dragon withdrew again some fifteen or twenty thousand years ago, man was on the verge of literacy. He already possessed great art, as the paintings in the Lascaux cavern reveal. It was an art devoted to the unseen, to the powers that control the movement of game and the magic that drives the hunter's shaft to its target. Without such magic man felt weak and helpless against the vagaries of nature. It was his first attempt at technology, at control of nature by dominating the luck element, the principle of uncertainty in the universe.

A few millennia farther on in time man had forgotten the doorway of snow through which he had emerged. He would only rediscover the traces of the ice age in the nineteenth century by means of the new science of geology. At first he would not believe his own history or the reality of the hidden ice dragon, even though Greenland and the polar world today lie shrouded beneath that same ice. He would not see that what the Eskimo said to Rasmussen was a belated modern enactment of an age-old drama in which we, too, had once participated. "We fear," the Eskimo sage had said in essence, "we fear the ice and cold. We fear nature which we do not understand and that provides us with food or brings famine."

Man achieving literacy on the far Mediterranean shores in an instant of golden sunlight would take the world as it was, to be forever. He would explore the intricacies of thought and wisdom in Athens. He would dream the first dreams of science and record them upon scrolls of parchment. Twenty-five centuries later those dreams would culminate in vast agricultural projects, green revolutions, power pouring through great pipelines, or electric energy surging across continents. Voices would speak into the distances of space. Hugh jet transports would hurtle through the skies. Radio telescopes would listen to cosmic whispers from beyond our galaxy. Enormous concentrations of people would gather and be fed in towering metropolises. Few would remember the Greek word *hubris*, the term for overweening pride, that pride which eventually causes some unseen balance to swing in the opposite direction.

Today the ice at the poles lies quiet. There have been times in the past when it has maintained that passivity scores of thousands of years—times longer, in fact, than the endurance of the whole of urban civilization since its first incipient beginnings no more than seven thousand years ago. The temperature gradient from the poles to the equator is still steeper than throughout much of the unglaciated periods of the past. The doorway through which man has come is just tentatively closing behind him.

So complex is the problem of the glacial rhythms that

no living scientist can say with surety the ice will not return. If it does the swarming millions who now populate the planet may mostly perish in misery and darkness, inexorably pushed from their own lands to be rejected in desperation by their neighbors. Like the devouring locust swarms that gather in favorable summers, man may have some of that same light-winged ephemeral quality about him. One senses it occasionally in those places where the dropped, transported boulders of the ice fields still hint of formidable powers lurking somewhere behind the face of present nature.

These fractured mementoes of devastating cold need to be contemplated for another reason than themselves. They constitute exteriorly what may be contemplated interiorly. They contain a veiled warning, perhaps the greatest symbolic warning man has ever received from nature. The giant fragments whisper, in the words of Einstein, that "nature does not always play the same game." Nature is devious in spite of what we have learned of her. The greatest scholars have always sensed this. "She will tell you a direct lie if she can," Charles Darwin once warned a sympathetic listener. Even Darwin, however, alert as he was to vestigial traces of former evolutionary structures in our bodies, was not in a position to foresee the kind of strange mental archaeology by which Sigmund Freud would probe the depths of the human mind. Today we are aware of the latent and shadowy powers contained in the subconscious: the alternating winter and sunlight of the human soul.

Has the earth's glacial winter, for all our mastery of science, surely subsided? No, the geologist would answer. We merely stand in a transitory spot of sunshine that takes on the illusion of permanence only because the human generations are short.

Has the wintry bleakness in the troubled heart of humanity at least equally retreated?—that aspect of man referred to when the Eskimo, adorned with amulets to ward off evil, reiterated: "Most of all we fear the secret misdoings of the heedless ones among ourselves."

No, the social scientist would have to answer, the winter of man has not departed. The Eskimo standing in the snow, when questioned about his beliefs, said: "We do not believe. We only fear. We fear those things which are about us and of which we have no sure knowledge . . . ."

But surely we can counter that this old man was an ignorant remnant of the ice age, fearful of a nature he did not understand. Today we have science, we do not fear the Eskimo's malevolent ghosts. We do not wear amulets to ward off evil spirits. We have pierced to the far rim of the universe. We roam mentally through light-years of time.

Yes, this could be admitted, but we also fear. We fear more deeply than the old man in the snow. It comes to us, if we are honest, that perhaps nothing has changed the grip of winter in our hearts, that winter before which we cringed amidst the ice long ages ago.

For what is it that we do? We fear. We do not fear ghosts but we fear the ghost of ourselves. We have come now, in this time, to fear the water we drink, the air we breathe, the insecticides that are dusted over our giant fruits. Because of the substances we have poured into our contaminated rivers we fear the food that comes to us from the sea. There are also those who tell us that by our own heedless acts the sea is dying.

We fear the awesome powers we have lifted out of nature and cannot return to her. We fear the weapons we have made, the hatreds we have engendered. We fear the crush of fanatic people to whom we readily sell these weapons. We fear for the value of the money in our pockets which stands symbolically for food and shelter. We fear the growing power of the state to take all these things from us. We fear to walk in our streets at evening. We have come to fear even our scientists and their gifts.

We fear, in short, as that self-sufficient Eskimo of the long night had never feared. Our minds, if not our clothes, are hung with invisible amulets: nostrums changed each year for our bodies whether it be chlorophyl toothpaste, the signs of astrology, or cold cures that do not cure: witchcraft nostrums for our society as it fractures into contending multitudes all crying for liberation without responsibility.

We fear, and never in this century will we cease to fear. We fear the end of man as that old shaman in the snow had never had cause to fear it. There is a winter still about us—the winter of man that has followed him relentlessly from the caverns and the ice. The old Eskimo spoke well. It is the winter of the heedless ones. We are in the winter. We have never left its breath.

Loren Eiseley is Benjamin Franklin Professor of Anthropology at the University of Pennsylvania, and the author of "The Invisible Pyramid."

The Hope of Man

By Loren Eiseley

PHILADELPHIA—Tomorrow the American people will make a decision; tomorrow a long-sought peace will be in process and a leader chosen. So deeply has our society been riven by conflict, however, so deep has grown the worry over the innumerable problems presented by our dinosaur cities and frenetic technology that we find ourselves still torn by dissension, cynicism and fear. With one foot poised at the threshold of the stars and with almost limitless power at our command we tremble over that which we have created.

Our youth have been alienated. Many of them avoid history and would place the evils from which they suffer upon their fathers' generation alone. Ethnic groups eye each other with distrust; venal politicians make promises that are impossible to keep. Waste multiplies and oceanographers whisper that the oceans themselves are dying, their vital food chains disrupted. Man, one historian ventures to write, will perish in poverty and darkness, as he began in misery and darkness.

Students and their elders come to the lecturers' platform and ask, some timidly, some defiantly, can there be any hope for man? Some turn away to immerse themselves in occult literature or read tarot cards; some reject the teacher before he has spoken. Almost without exception we have come to believe that the future is something one comes upon like a venomous serpent under a rock; namely, that one can exercise no power over it or avoid its fangs. In this common belief there exists a dreadful half-truth.

Some 350 years ago, in the spectral half-morning of science, a great statesman and uncannily perceptive philosopher, Sir Francis Bacon, wrote as follows:

"I am now therefore to speak touching hope. It is fit that I make hope in this matter reasonable." There is no record of Bacon's funeral. The titled and educated shrugged and dismissed his ideas. In Britain, the twentieth century was well-nigh reached before universities were modeled along the lines he had conceived.

What then was it of which Bacon spoke? He spoke of science, of the examination of nature, of learning to live by her laws and diverting her powers for human benefit, but he wrote in an age which, if not precisely like our own, brooded in a similar darksome folly. It believed in a world far gone in decay, and nearing its end—an autumn world. Its eyes were cast backward upon the great classical civilizations which men never hope to equal.

Through this Elizabethan Age of violence and the headsman's axe, Bacon walked cool, masked and remote, "a stranger" in his own time. But the stranger wrote with such axiomatic brevity that a generation or two after his death he influenced the founding of the Royal Society and the style of English letters. His thinking crossed the western ocean and affected the American school system. Slowly the autumnal smell of decay passed from men's minds. The West began to learn from Bacon's half-forgotten writings what he had termed the "invention of inventions," the scientific method itself, with all the multiplying wonders it had promised.

"This is the foundation of all," he had written to his mostly unbelieving and deaf audience, "for we are not to imagine or suppose but to *discover* what nature does or may be made to do." To men lost in the cobwebs of religious fanaticism and Aristotelian logic the words so readily acceptable today had been dismissed as the vaporings of a fool.

Hope? Yes, he had given it and in time it had been remembered. Scientific organizations had arisen modeled upon his words. There came, in time, canals, bridges, railways, lights, voices traveling invisibly upon wires, and then passing, like invisible ghosts, into space: Diseases were conquered, and then there approached, in the twentieth century, that deathly triumph in which the power to destroy the world pulsed in men's hands.

Francis Bacon, whose insight over three centuries ago had pierced the future, began to be cursed as having called up that which could not be laid: a soaring population, the bleakness and grime of great factories, the violence of alienation, the deathly air fleets, the insecticides and sewage pouring down to the sea, the discovery that we were a sand grain planet floating in a galaxial wheel that light itself took over a hundred thousand years to cross. Hope? Where was it now?

Forgotten was Bacon's other dictum written long before the rise of the city of dreadful night that represented, in nineteenth-century Britain, the apotheosis of the industrial state. Those who will not attend these matters, the far-sighted time voyager had anticipated, "neither win the kingdom of nature nor govern it."

He was saying, in other words, that the future is not come upon lying in the street. It is drawn from our own substance. Bacon had told us how to live with nature, to create that *mundus alter*, that other better, more serene world that can be drawn from nature by human effort. Have a care in the way you treat her, he had cautioned, you do not master nature, you live with her laws and adjust to them. She contains the powers of the hurricane, of the great swells that rising from the seabed overwhelm the cities of the shore.

Hope? He had hope, but in him it was always allied to a statesman's wisdom. It had to be tempered with human humility that sees "a farre off even that which is future." Systems analysis, we are just beginning to call it.

"Oh, very well," counter the modern critics. Perhaps in the beginning science saved lives, reduced superstition, taught us our place in the universe, even traced our origins to a quivering tree shrew on a branch. Science delved through layers of neocortex and found the noisome sewage growing below the conscious mind. I say to you what is the relevance of the earth past, what is the relevance of evolution if all it can reveal is the mind that devises napalm and the brutal efficiencies of the concentration camp? Answer me, speak to me about hope, if you can. Bacon may have dreamed, but his *mundus alter* has gone astray. It is not the world he dreamed.

"Agreed, it is not the world he dreamed," I have murmured upon many a platform, but, I repeat, he warned it must be drawn from human substance. Let me try to tell you what that substance is, for only so can we repeat Bacon's wistful phrase about science as touching upon hope.

The word "crisis" is indeed formidable but it should not be confined to this century which has popularized it. The whole history of man has been a crisis. Ten million years, in fact, have elapsed between the first mandible whose tooth alignment and structure could vaguely be called human, and the fall of the first bomb upon Hiroshima. Man has survived the great continental glaciers which turned most of the Northern Hemisphere into an ice desert. He has lived on while the giant herbivores of the terminal ice melted away with the last glaciers.

He turned to wild grains as his final recourse against famine. In doing so he engendered another crisis: he would raise the spectre of famine and disease as it never before had been experienced upon earth. Like an Oriental djinn he would start the blowing of dust and the making of deserts which would not be laid within our time. Populations originally dispersed would, with mounting energy at their disposal, concentrate in cities.

The Black Death which descended upon Europe in 1348 was more devastating in its time than any bomb so far released. There was no antidote. Perhaps as high as a third of the population of West Europe perished. When the disease passed, the feudal system lay in ruins. The Black Death was the soundest challenge, a warning out of that old unregenerate nature capable of the vast sea swells and turbulence of which the great Elizabethan was later to warn.

I have said man's entire career has been a crisis and he has survived by mother wit. Huddled in a cave in the middle Ice Age, suppose that a group of half-human man apes had dreamed throatily of the future by a leaping fire? Would they have had a word for hope that extended beyond next day's hunting? Would they have foreseen the stone in the hand changed to the arrow's leap across space? Would they have ever foreseen the booklined room in which I am writing, or the murmurous history of great minds talking across the centuries?

I think not. I am not even sure they hoped, but they did more than seek survival. They risked. They risked the mounting of the first wild stallion, they risked their lives on water. They eyed for long centuries the air and mastered it. They crossed the poles amidst new death. They have now risked the moon. There are even those among them who risk love and compassion across the boundaries of race and form, men who risk the very love of earth itself and would protect for the sake of those unborn.

This touches upon hope, the hope of a crisis animal who risks and gives himself to good; to good causes and to bad, but who risks, risks always against the future. It was Bacon who uttered the final warning, but to me, paradoxically, it constitutes the final hope. He said: "Nature is more violent in the Returne."

Man is a part of nature. In the creation of his second world he sometimes forgets, as now, and a foulness follows him. It is not the first time. But survival is secondary in man to risk. If he has been violent in his wars, he has been also ennobled by compassion.

Students ask about hope and I repeat as that great seer before me: Nature is most violent in the return. Man is nature's child. He has come a tremendous journey across time, a crisis journey. I believe that of those swells and violence of which Bacon took account in nature, man's love for earth may be more "violent in the returne" than we can presently understand. In some it is already a love responding to all earth's creatures, a love that seeks to direct Bacon's second world along the ignored road the great Elizabethan charted. I conceive it as humanity's last great tidal swell in human nature. I have sensed it dimly, wistfully in some of our own youth, the so-called flower people. I have sensed it in those lonely sentinels of the centuries, Lao-Tze, the Buddha and the Christ.

It has been said that the way of man is not in himself, but the man who said it did not forecast Bacon's five great words appended to his definition of science, "for the uses of life." That is the hope and the risk and the effort that began ten million years ago when the first men crouched in the shelter of a forest tree and trembled before their unknown journey. Risk and hope began then; risk, terrible risk, and hope that continues to this hour.

We are a free nation seeking our own way beyond and above our great machines. Let the mountain wave, Bacon's final prophecy, be that of compassion, not of hate. It contains the risk, the final risk for which man was conceived and shaped in the dark caverns of the past. He was born a crisis animal; it is his destiny. There confronts him now, hope for earth's frail web of life, or that choice of cold indifference which leads to the pathway of no return.

Hope and risk, are they too great to expect of man? I do not believe it. They constitute his shadow. They have followed him for a million years. They stood with him at the Hot Gates of Thermopylae. They shared the cross at Calvary. I think it was really there that the great wave began to gather when all else seemed lost. We are again threatened with the insidious Elizabethan malady of weariness. But a voice spoke then of hope, and of great reversals, of impending tides. May this too be such an age. May Francis Bacon's voice still speak of hope, not for man only, but of the survival of the planetary life without which our own lives are as nothing. The risk is there but the indomitable human spirit will cry "assume the risk." By it alone has man survived. And only those who know what it is to risk can understand compassion.

Freedom and Dignity Revisited

By B. F. Skinner

CAMBRIDGE, Mass.—In a famous passage in "Notes From the Underground" Dostoevski insisted that man will never admit that his behavior can be predicted and controlled. He will "create destruction and chaos to gain his point. And if all this could in turn be analyzed and prevented by predicting that it would occur, then man would deliberately go mad to prove his point." Dostoevski was himself making a prediction, of course, and it had the curious effect of cutting off this last avenue of escape, since henceforth even deliberately going mad could be said to have been predicted.

My critics have, nevertheless, seemed bent on proving that he was right. Many of them have shown a taste for destruction and chaos, some of it not far short of madness. They have resorted to highly emotional terms, and a kind of hysterical blindness seems to have prevented some of them from reading what I actually wrote. An author who has been so widely misunderstood will naturally value Dostoevski's explanation.

My argument was surely simple enough. I was not discussing a philosophical entity called freedom but rather the behavior of those who struggle to be free. It is part of the human genetic endowment that when a person acts in such a way as to reduce "aversive" (e.g., potentially dangerous) stimuli, he is more likely to do so again. Thus, when other people attempt to control him through a threat of punishment, he learns to escape from them or attack them in order to weaken their power. When he succeeds, he feels free, and the struggle ceases. But is he really free? To say with John Stuart Mill, that "liberty consists in doing what one desires" is to neglect the determiners of desires. There are certain kinds of control under which people feel perfectly free. The point has been made before, but I was offering some further evidence recently acquired in the experimental analysis of operant conditioning.

Such an interpretation is not metaphysics; it is a matter of identifying certain processes in an important field of human behavior. It does not—it cannot—lead to the suppression of any freedom we have ever enjoyed. On the contrary, it suggests that there are ways in which we could all feel freer than ever before. For example, in spite of our supposed love of freedom, most of our practices in government, education, psychotherapy and industry are still heavily punitive. People behave in given ways to avoid the consequences of not doing so. Perhaps this means simply that the struggle for freedom has not yet been finished, but I have argued that the continuing use of punishment is, on the contrary, an unwanted by-product of that struggle. We refuse to accept nonpunitive practices because they make it too clear that control is being exerted. When we punish bad behavior, we can give the individual credit for behaving well, but if we arrange conditions under which he "desires" to behave well, the conditions must get the credit.

I neglected to point out that under punitive practices we even justify behaving badly. Fortunately, this has now been done for me by the film "A Clockwork Orange." Writing in The New York Review, Christopher Ricks argues that aversion therapy takes the protagonist Alex "beyond freedom and dignity," and he quotes Anthony Burgess (author of the novel) in defense of the film. "What my, and Kubrick's [director of the film] parable tries to state is that it is preferable to have a world of violence undertaken in full awareness—violence chosen as an act of will—than a world conditioned to be good or harmless." Ricks says that I am one of the few who would contest that statement. I hope there are far more than a few. The film misrepresents the issue because the "therapy" that makes Alex good is brutally conspicuous while the conditioning that lies behind his "acts of will undertaken in full awareness" is easily missed.

The struggle for freedom has not reduced or eliminated control; it has merely corrected it. But what is good control, and who is to exert it? Either my answers to these questions have been unforgivably obscure or many of my critics have not reached the last chapters in my book. The question Who will control? is not to be answered with a proper name or by describing a kind of person (e.g. a benevolent dictator) or his qualifications (e.g. a behavioral engineer). To do so is to make the mistake of looking at the person rather than at the environment which determines his behavior. The struggle for freedom has moved slowly, and alas erratically, toward a culture in which controlling power is less and less likely to fall into the hands of individuals or groups who use it tyrannically. We have tried to construct such a culture by exerting countercontrol over those who misuse power. Countercontrol is certainly effective, but it leads at best to a kind of uneasy equilibrium. The next step can be taken only through the explicit design of a culture which goes beyond the immediate interests of controller and countercontroller.

Design for what? There is only one answer: the survival of the culture and of mankind. Survival is a difficult value (compared, say, with life, liberty or the pursuit of happiness) because it is hard to predict the conditions a culture must meet, and we are only beginning to understand how to produce the behavior needed to meet them. Moreover, we are likely to reject survival as a value because it suggests competition with other cultures, as in social Darwinism, in which aggressive behavior is aggrandized, but other contingencies of survival are important, and the value of cooperative, supportive behavior can easily be demonstrated.

Must individual freedoms be "sacrificed" for the sake of the culture? Most of my critics contend that I am saying so, but the answer depends on how people are induced to work for the good of their culture. If they do so under a threat of punishment, then freedom (from such a threat) is sacrificed, but if they are induced to do so through positive reinforcement, their sense of freedom is enhanced. Young Chinese wear plain clothing, live in crowded quarters, eat simple diets, observe a rather puritanical sexual code and work long hours—all for the greater glory of China. Are they sacrificing any freedom? They are if they are under

aversive control, if they behave as they do because they will be denounced by their fellows when they behave otherwise. But if Mao has succeeded in making signs of progress toward a greater China positively reinforcing, then it is possible that they feel freer, and happier, than most young Americans.

Misunderstanding no doubt arises from the word "control." Dostoevski used the metaphor of a piano key: strike it, and it responds with a given tone. The metaphor was appropriate to the early reflexology of Dostoevski's time, which Pavlov's conditioned reflexes did little to change. But in operant conditioning a stimulus merely alters the likelihood that a response will be emitted. Good examples are to be found in verbal behavior. A verbal response is very different from the knee-jerk elicited by a tap on the patellar tendon. What a speaker says is determined in part by the current listener, in part by the recent verbal stimuli he has heard or seen, in part by a nonverbal setting, and in large part of course by his history as listener and speaker. These variables can be sorted out by identifying well-established behavioral processes.

There was an excellent example of the probabilistic control exerted by verbal stimulus at a recent symposium at Yale University organized to discuss "Beyond Freedom and Dignity." On the second evening, several students brought in a large banner reading "Remember the Air War," which they hung from the balcony. It could not be seen by many in the audience, but it confronted the five panelists on the platform throughout the evening. It had a predictable effect: Everyone of us mentioned the war in Vietnam at some point in his discussion and the last speaker, Sir Denis Brogan, put aside his manuscript and spoke only of the war.

That was good behavioral engineering. We should learn to live with it.

B. F. Skinner, author of "Beyond Freedom and Dignity," is professor of psychology at Harvard.

The Limited Pool of Human Talent

By C. D. Darlington

OXFORD, England—If we bring up children, our own or other people's, we soon notice that they differ not only in appearance but also in behavior and abilities. They differ in what they can learn and also in what they want to learn—mentally or manually. On the mental side they differ even in how they learn the same thing whether it is by sound or sight or symbol. A whole range of consequences follow. They differ in how they remember and use what they have learned and hence in the skills they acquire. They differ consequently in their curiosity and initiative, in their amusements and sense of humor, and, above all, in their credulity, in the beliefs about the world around them, scientific or superstitious, which they are willing to accept.

From this experience of human differences we usually, and I think reasonably, conclude that human beings are individuals.

Is individuality then a matter of heredity? Here we have to clear up a very widespread misunderstanding. Brothers and sisters have the same ancestry. But, in an outbred society like ours, brothers and sisters differ in their heredity. This is because they, or most of them, have four different grandparents and eight different great-grandparents whose heredity is differently, sometimes very differently, distributed to them. But environment is another matter. Their environments are usually as like as their parents can make them. From which we can conclude that their differences of character must be due to their differences of heredity.

These differences between brothers can be striking enough. But the differences between nonbrothers are obviously greater. Can we also discover how much of these are due to heredity and how much to environment? We can do so by comparing the intelligence and behavior of foundlings or of adopted children taken into a single home. When we apply intelligence tests we find there is a correlation between the scores of the children and of their real parents whom they have never known. Further, when we ask adoption societies how they place their children, they say they have to avoid over-placing, that is, putting a child with foster parents who are socially and mentally too far above the natural parents.

In asking such questions we cannot go very far without facing the problems of social class. In Western European countries for thirty or forty generations there has been a systematic attempt to catch bright boys wherever they could be found in order to train them to be "clerks," men who would be useful in administration. It has long been a source of astonishment that the Doomsday Survey of England was completed in December, 1085, in less than two years.

There is much evidence of this. If we look carefully, for example, at Shakespeare's plays we see a picture of class differences as he saw them. The picture that Shakespeare draws is convincing. Indeed we find very little difficulty in applying it to our own day in England. In Shakespeare's time only a small fraction of the people were taught to read and write. And today almost all children are compelled to go to school for ten years to learn these things. Free and compulsory education for three generations has failed to produce the leveling effect that was often expected of it.

Does this then mean that compulsory education has had no effect? Far from it. It has transformed all social classes but not in a way that was foreseen. The working classes in England a century ago contained a large minority of men and women thirsting for knowledge, thirsting for the opportunities of a literate and technical education which the social system had prevented them from enjoying. Their children did profit by it. Partly through the trade unions, and partly through the educational system itself, they moved up into the professional classes. They enriched society as a whole. But their promotion impoverished the class they had left behind them.

It had been thought that the reservoir of talent in the working classes was unlimited or at least inexhaustible. It was necessary only to increase the opportunities of higher education for these opportunities to be seized by a fraction of each succeeding generation. But we now find that the supply of new talent is diminishing. It is no longer equal to the supply of new education. The newly expanded universities have to rely largely on the talent that was already visible in the preceding generation.

England is only a small example of a principle which has been operating throughout the history of man—and, indeed, if we care to follow the story back so far, throughout his evolution. It is the principle that whenever an invention has been made, brains prove to be in short supply. The reason? Because every new invention demands new abilities to use and develop it. Every new invention has therefore added to the advantage of those individuals and classes and races who by nature (and by heredity) possess such abilities. It has also added and will continue to add to the disadvantage of those who do not possess them.

C. D. Darlington of Oxford University is one of the world's foremost biologists.

Beyond Contemporary Consciousness

By William Irwin Thompson

ANALOGY ONE: Imagine insects with a life span of two weeks, and then imagine that they are trying to build up a science about the nature of time and history. Clearly, they haven't seen enough of the seasons to build a model on the basis of a few days of summer. So let us endow them with a language and a culture through which they can pass on their knowledge to future generations. Summer passes, then autumn, and finally it is winter. The winter insects are a whole new breed and have perfected a new and revolutionary science on the basis of the "hard facts" of their perceptions of snow. As for the myths and legends of summer: clearly, the intelligent insects are not going to believe the superstitions of their primitive ancestors.

ANALOGY TWO: Imagine a vehicle as large as a planet that began a voyage an eon ago. After generations of voyaging, the mechanics lose all sense of who they are and where they are going. They begin to grow unhappy with their condition and say that the notion that they are on a journey in an enormous vehicle is a myth put forth by the ruling class to disguise its oppression of the mechanical class. There is a revolution; the Captain is killed, but some of the star-men escape in a smaller shuttle craft. Elated, they proclaim the dictatorship of the proletariat and have all the records of the Captain's log destroyed, for these, they claim, are nothing but the lies of the old ruling class.

These analogies indicate that information is subject to decay through time. There is a half-life to cosmic myth, as Vico realized in a different way two hundred years ago. An epoch begins with a divine consciousness of a cosmic myth in the Age of Gods, but by the time of the following Age of Heroes, half the myth is gone, and with it, half the divine consciousness; by the time of the Age of Men, myth and consciousness halve again, leaving only a quarter of the original.

Finally, in the ultimate age of barbarism and chaos, nothing remains of the original myth and divine consciousness at all; but as entropy reaches its limit in chaos, there is a reversal in the cycle, an inverse entropy, in which chaos creates the fertile decay for a new cosmic myth and a new Age of Gods. We spiral back to the past in a future on a higher level of order. Readers of The New York Times will recognize that we are indeed living in an age of chaos.

But to understand the nature of the chaos of our particular historical moment, we have to move far away from our immediate and confining present. Cultural transformations are so large that they are invisible to individuals who are only concerned with practical day-to-day business. If you went around in England in 1770 asking people how it felt to be living in an age of Industrial Revolution, most people would not know what you were talking about. But if you went to see the "lunatic" William Blake living in obscurity, he would tell you about the meaning of the great cultural transformation by moving back and forth from one end of history to the other in a notation especially designed for ideas so large, that is, mythology. Events that are too large to be perceived in immediate history register in the unconscious in the collective form of myth, and since artists and visionaries possess a strong mytho-poeic imagination, they can express in the microcosm of their works what is going on in the macrocosm of mankind.

Because the imagination can outrace economic or technological development, ideologies can be elaborated in advance of their social need. In 1770 the Scottish Primitivists developed a theory, contrary to the Biblical account, that men evolved from woodmen to land-dwellers to settled city-dwellers. This vision of progress was quite different from the Christian notion of The Fall, yet it was precisely this vision of progress that became the ideology of Industrial England by the time of the Great Exhibition of 1851. Similarly, William Blake understood the implications of industrialization better than his contemporaries. From a few eighteenth century brick kilns he was able to extrapolate imaginatively the complete transformation of human society.

Imaginative artists like Blake can understand the collective condition of society because the imagination is itself the opening to the collective unconscious; and precisely because this consciousness is collective, imaginative people can think the same thought at the same time even though they are separated by ordinary space. No one blew a whistle in Europe in 1760 and said: "Stop thinking neoclassically; start thinking romantically in terms of primitives and nature." And yet the whole age did shift dramatically. Because we do not understand this process, we either ignore it or use vague terms like "spirit of the age." Hegel would call it the *Weltgeist*, but whatever term is used the radical implication is that the human mind is not contained by the skull.

The unconscious is not personal. Behavioral psychologists, bringing up the rear with the dead mechanistic science of the eighteenth century, would assert that culture operates only through social interactions; for them space separates and what does not touch physically or symbolically can have no effect upon anything.

Physicists once thought the universe was like a black void containing bits of stuff colliding in Brownian motion; now they assert that all is energy and vibration and that the solar wind reaches to the limits of the solar system. When the sun, moon, and earth line up in an eclipse, magnetic perturbations give us earthquakes like a recent one in Los Angeles. All of which sounds as if we have spiraled back on a higher level of order to the astronomy of Stonehenge, circa 1750 B. C. If we can spiral back astronomically to the archaic world view, we can also spiral back to it psychologically to realize that the mind of mankind is a collective and interpenetrating field.

The unconscious is not personal, but in order not to be swamped by infinite information, the brain functions as what Aldous Huxley called "a reducing valve," and shuts out the universe so that the individual can do what is in front of him. The million signals a second must be reduced to a few. But the creative intuition and the imagination maintain an opening to the unconscious, and this unconscious is outside the ordinary space-time of the brain. In the relativistic space-time of the unconscious the past and the future mysteriously interpenetrate in exactly the way the ancient Maya understood in their fantastic calendar of millions of years of cyclical, spiraling time.

The priestly hierarchy of ancient Mexico knew that this planet earth was an enormous vehicle moving through infinite expanses of space-time. In the temples the priests kept the records of who we were, where we came from, and where we were going; but as the cosmic myth decayed through time, the distance between the decadent priesthood and the oppressed peasantry increased. The peasants rose up, attacked and then abandoned the ceremonial centers, and lowered their horizons from the stars to only what was in front of them.

Because ancient Mexico is not part of our general awareness, artists have to speak to us in a different mythology. Blake was one attempt, Yeats another. But these mythological ideas are not always expressed with genius. An idea in the collective unconscious is what Lévi-Strauss would call a *structure*, but when that structure is performed in an individual's consciousness it takes on the limitations of the personal *content*.

The mythical message from the collective unconscious must travel through the distorting medium of culture and the individual before it reaches the receiver. The myth plus the noise from the distorting medium is what reaches the receiver; so in order to be sure he has the message right he has to listen to several different variations until he grasps the structure. In the cases of some individuals who transmit mythical information, there is more noise than anything else. If one lines up the science fiction novels of C. S. Lewis, Arthur C. Clarke, and Doris Lessing; scholarly works like Shklovskii and Sagan's "Intelligent Life in the Universe," my own "At the Edge of History," and potboilers like van Daniken's "Chariot of the Gods," he can see that the range of information-plus-noise varies considerably. Nevertheless the *structure* of a new planetary consciousness is definitely in evidence in each work, no matter what its literary or scholarly merit may be.

What the new planetary consciousness indicates is that something has already happened in the collective unconsciousness of mankind. The movement of humanism that began with the Renaissance is at an end and a new ideology is being created in advance of its social need. What particular institutional form this consciousness will take no one can say.

One cannot infer the Crystal Palace of the Great Exhibition of 1851 from the vision of progress of the Scottish Primitivists of 1770. But one can take a few guesses. I would guess that the new planetary consciousness means that we are building up a larger model of reality in which religious myth and scientific fact are both simultaneously true. Clearly, this will amount to a scientific revolution as large as that of the sixteenth century. In "The Structure of Scientific Revolutions," T. S. Kuhn says that " . . . at times of revolution, when the normal-scientific tradition changes, the scientist's perception of his environment must be re-educated—in some familiar situations he must learn to see a new *gestalt*." To see a *gestalt* is not to analyze things visually in pieces, but to have a vision.

William Irwin Thompson is author of "At the Edge of History," and director of the Lindisfarne Association.

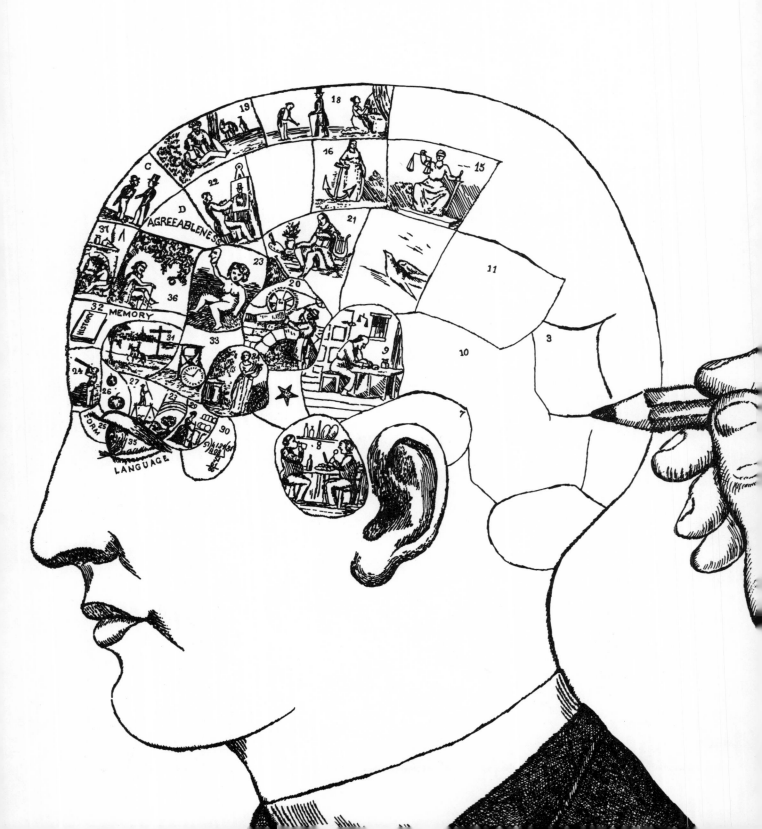

Washington's 'Problem-Solvers'—

Where They Went Wrong By Hannah Arendt

The Pentagon Papers—a richly documented record of the American role in Indochina from World War II to May 1968—tell different stories, teach different lessons to different readers. Some claim they have only now understood that Vietnam was the "logical" outcome of the cold war or the anti-Communist ideology, others that this is a unique opportunity to learn about decision-making processes in government, but most readers have by now agreed that the basic issue raised is deception.

The famous credibility gap has suddenly opened up into an abyss. The quicksand of lying statements of all sorts, deceptions as well as self-deception, is apt to engulf any reader who wishes to probe this material, which, unhappily, he must recognize as the infrastructure of nearly a decade of United States foreign and domestic policy.

Because of the extravagant lengths to which the commitment to nontruthfulness in politics went on at the highest level of government, and because of the concomitant extent to which lying was permited to proliferate throughout the ranks of all governmental services, military and civilian—the phony body counts of the "search-and-destroy" missions, the doctored after-damage reports of the Air Force, the "progress" reports to Washington from the field written by subordinates who knew that their performance would be evaluated by their own reports—one is easily tempted to forget the background of past history, itself not exactly a story of immaculate virtue, against which this newest episode must be seen and judged.

To the many genres in the art of lying developed in the past, we must now add two more recent varieties. There is, *first*, the apparently innocuous one of the public relations managers in government who learned their trade from the inventiveness of Madison Avenue. Public relations is but a variety of advertising; hence it has it origin in the consumer society, with its inordinate appetite for goods to be distributed through a market economy. The trouble with the mentality of the public relations man is that he deals only in opinions and "goodwill," the readiness to buy, that is, in intangibles whose concrete reality is at a minimum.

It is not surprising that the recent generation of intellectuals, who grew up in the insane atmosphere of rampant advertising and were taught that half of politics is "image-making" and the other half the art of making people believe in the imagery, should almost automatically fall back on the older adages of carrot and stick whenever the situation becomes too serious for "theory." To them the greatest disappointment in the Vietnam adventure should have been the discovery that there are people with whom carrot-and-stick methods do not work either.

The *second* new variety of the art of lying, though less frequently met with in everyday life, plays a more important role in the Pentagon Papers. It also appeals to much better men, to those, for example, who are likely to be found in the higher ranks of the civilian services. They are, in Neil Sheehan's felicitous phrase, professional "problem-solvers," and they were drawn into government from the universities and the various think tanks, some of them equipped with game theories and systems analyses, thus prepared, as they thought, to solve all the "problems" of foreign policy.

The problem-solvers have been characterized as men of great self-confidence, who "seem rarely to doubt their ability to prevail," and they worked together with the members of the military of whom "the history remarks that they were 'men accustomed to winning.' " We should not forget that we owe it to the problem-solvers' effort at impartial self-examination, rare among such people, that the actors' attempts at hiding their role behind a screen of self-protective secrecy (at least until they have completed their memoirs—in our century the most deceitful genre of literature) were frustrated. The basic integrity of those who wrote the report is beyond doubt; they could indeed be trusted by Secretary McNamara to produce an "encyclopedic and objective" report and "to let the chips fall where they may."

But these moral qualities, which deserve admiration, clearly did not prevent them from participating for many years in the game of deceptions and falsehoods. Confident "of place, of education and accomplishment," they lied perhaps out of a mistaken patriotism. But the point is that they lied not so much for their country—certainly not for their country's survival, which was never at stake—as for its "image." In spite of their undoubted intelligence—it is manifest in many memos from their pens—they also believed that politics is but a variety of public relations, and they were taken in by all the bizarre psychological premises underlying this belief.

Washington's "problem-solvers" obviously were different from the ordinary image-makers. Their distinction lies in that they were problem-solvers as well. Hence they were not just intelligent, but prided themselves on being "rational," and they were indeed to a rather frightening degree above "sentimentality" and in love with "theory," the world of sheer mental effort. They were eager to find formulas, preferably expressed in a pseudomathematical language, that would unify the most disparate phenomena with which reality presented them; that is, they were eager to discover *laws* by which to explain and predict political and historical facts as though they were as necessary, and thus as reliable, as the physicists once believed natural phenomena to be.

The ultimate aim was neither power nor profit. Nor was it even influence in the world in order to serve particular, tangible interests for the sake of which prestige, an image of the "greatest power in the world," was needed and purposefully used. The goal was now the image itself, as is manifest in the very language of the problem-solvers, with their "scenarios" and "audiences," borrowed from the theater. For this ultimate aim, all policies became short-term interchangeable means, until finally, when all signs pointed to defeat in the war of attrition, the goal was no longer one of avoiding humiliating defeat but of finding ways and means to avoid admitting it and "save face."

Image-making as global policy—not world conquest, but victory in the battle "to win the people's minds"—is indeed something new in the huge arsenal of human follies recorded in history. This was not undertaken by a third-rate nation always apt to boast in order to compensate for the real thing, or by one of the old colonial powers that lost their position as a result of World War II and might have been tempted, as de Gaulle was, to bluff their way back to pre-eminence, but by "the dominant power."

In the case of the Vietnam war we are confronted with, in addition to falsehoods and confusion, a truly amazing and entirely honest ignorance of the historically pertinent background: Not only did the decision-makers seem ignorant of all the well-known facts of the Chinese revolution and the decade-old rift between Moscow and Peking that

preceded it, but no one at the top knew or considered it important that the Vietnamese had been fighting foreign invaders for almost 2,000 years, or that the notion of Vietnam as a "tiny backward nation" without interest to "civilized" nations, which is, unhappily, often shared by the war critics, stands in flagrant contradiction to the very old and highly developed culture of the region. What Vietnam lacks is not "culture," but strategic importance, a suitable terrain for modern mechanized armies, and rewarding targets for the Air Force. What caused the disastrous defeat of American policies and armed intervention was indeed no quagmire but the willful, deliberate disregard of all facts, historical, political, geographical, for more than twenty-five years.

The first explanation that comes to mind to answer the question "How could they?" is likely to point to the interconnectedness of deception and self-deception. In the contest between public statements, always overoptimistic, and the truthful reports of the intelligence community, persistently bleak and ominous, the public statements were liable to win simply because they were public. The great advantage of publicly established and accepted propositions over whatever an individual might secretly know or believe to be the truth is neatly illustrated by a medieval anecdote according to which a sentry, on duty to watch and warn the townspeople of the enemy's approach, jokingly sounded a false alarm—and then was the last to rush to the walls to defend the town against his invented enemies. From this, one may conclude that the more successful a liar is, the more people he has convinced, the more likely it is that he will end by believing his own lies.

In the Pentagon Papers we are confronted with people who did their utmost to win the minds of the people, that is, to manipulate them; but since they labored in a free country, where all kinds of information were available, they never really succeeded. Because of their relatively high station and their position in government, they were better shielded—in spite of their privileged knowledge of "top secrets"—against this public information, which also more or less told the factual truth, than were those whom they tried to convince and of whom they were likely to think in terms of mere audiences, "silent majorities," who were supposed to watch the scenarists' productions.

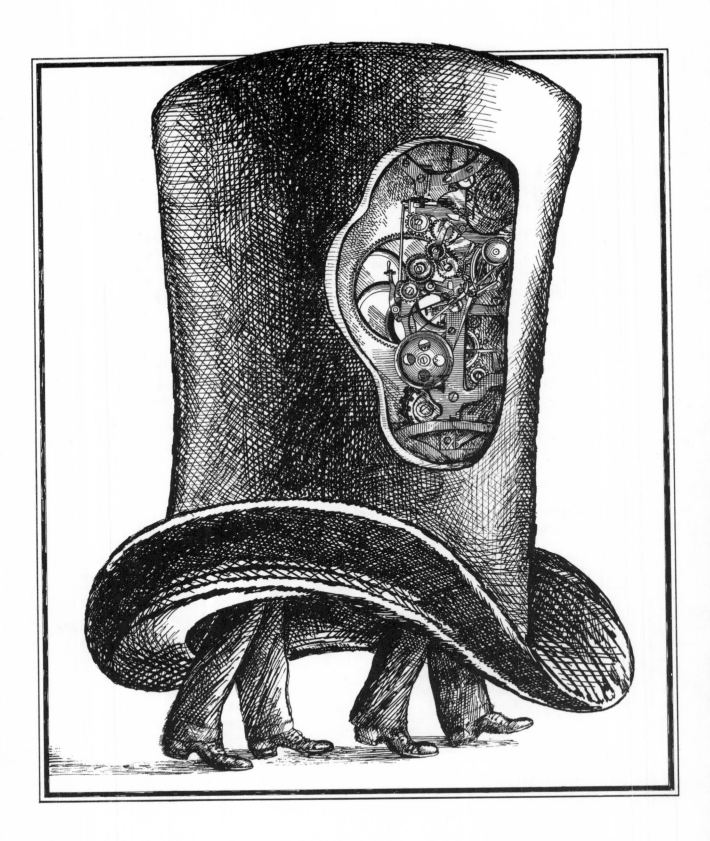

44

The internal world of government, with its bureaucracy on one hand, its social life on the other, made self-deception relatively easy. No ivory tower of the scholars has ever better prepared the mind for ignoring the facts of life than did the various think tanks for the problem-solvers and the reputation of the White House for the President's advisers. It was in this atmosphere, where defeat was less feared than admitting defeat, that the misleading statements about the disasters of the Tet offensive and the Cambodian invasion were concocted. But what is even more important is that the truth about such decisive matters could be successfully covered up in these internal circles—but nowhere else—by worries about how to avoid becoming "the first American President to lose a war" and by the always present preoccupations with the next election.

The problem-solvers, who lost their minds because they trusted the calculating powers of their brains at the expense of the mind's capacity for experience and its ability to learn from it, were preceded by the ideologists of the cold war period. Anti-Communism—not the old, often prejudiced hostility of America against Socialism and Communism, so strong in the twenties and still a mainstay of the Republican party during the Roosevelt Administration, but the postwar comprehensive ideology—was originally the brain child of former Communists who needed a new ideology by which to explain and reliably foretell the course of history. This ideology was at the root of all "theories" in Washington since the end of World War II.

This brings us to the root of the matter that, at least partially, might contain the answer to the question, How could they not only start these policies but carry them through to their bitter and absurd end? Defactualization and problem-solving were welcomed because disregard of reality was inherent in the policies and goals themselves. What did they have to know about Indochina as it really was, when it was no more than a "test case" or a domino, or a means to "contain China" or prove that we *are* the mightiest of the superpowers? Or take the case of bombing North Vietnam for the ulterior purpose of building morale in South Vietnam, without much intention of winning a clear-cut victory and ending the war. How could they be interested in anything as real as victory when they kept the war going not for territorial gain or economic advantage, least of all to help a friend or keep a commitment, and not even for the reality, as distinguished from the image, of power?

When this stage of the game was reached, the initial premise that we should never mind the region or the country itself—inherent in the domino theory—changed into "never mind the enemy." And this in the midst of a war! The result was that the enemy, poor, abused and suffering, grew stronger while "the mightiest country" grew weaker with each passing year.

The aspects of the Pentagon Papers that I have chosen, the aspects of deception, self-deception, image-making, ideologizing, and defactualization, are by no means the only features of the papers that deserve to be studied and learned from. There is, for instance, the fact that this massive and systematic effort at self-examination was commissioned by one of the chief actors, that 36 men could be found to compile the documents and write their analysis, quite a few of whom "had helped to develop or to carry out the policies they were asked to evaluate," that one of the authors, when it had become apparent that no one in government was willing to use or even read the results, went to the public and leaked it to the press, and that, finally, the most respectable newspapers in the country dared to bring material that was stamped "top secret" to the widest possible attention.

It has rightly been said by Neil Sheehan that Robert McNamara's decision to find out what went wrong, and why, "may turn out to be one of the most important decisions in his seven years at the Pentagon." It certainly restored, at least for a fleeting moment, this country's reputation in the world. What had happened could indeed hardly have happened anywhere else. It is as though all these people, involved in an unjust war and rightly compromised by it, had suddenly remembered what they owed to their forefathers' decent respect for the opinions of mankind.

©1971, Hannah Arendt

Hannah Arendt is a teacher and historian. This article is abridged from an essay, "Lying in Politics," in her book, "Crisis of the Republic."

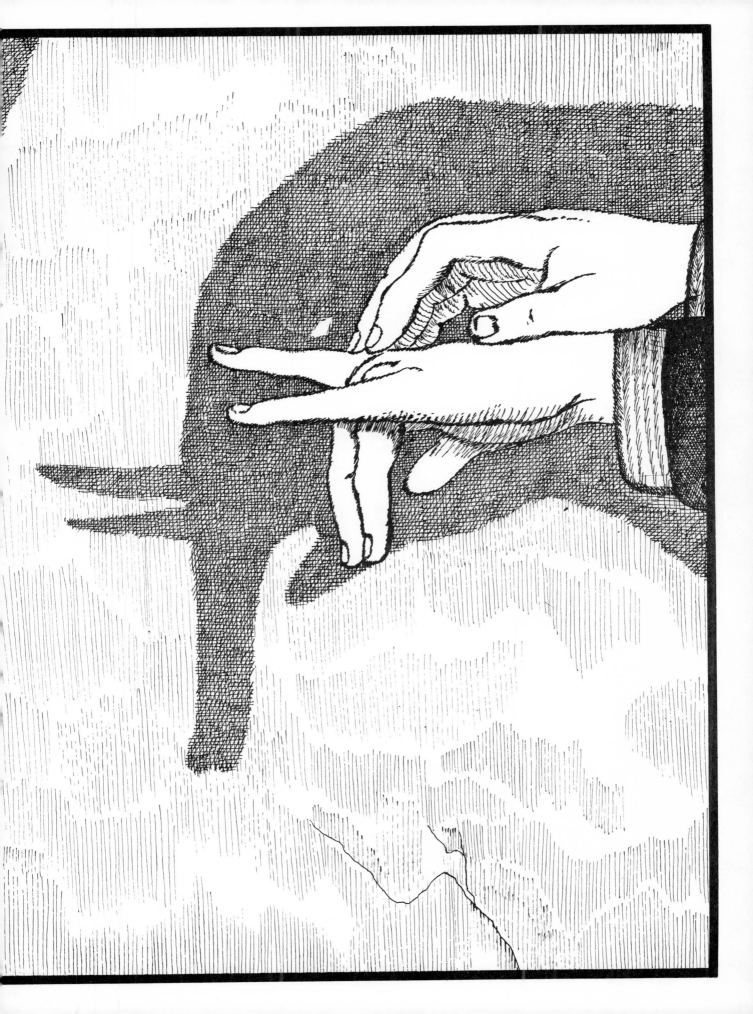

The Presidency:
Too Soon to Love Again

By Priscilla McMillan

CAMBRIDGE, Mass.—Presidential politics, for many of us, has become an area of life cordoned off by shock, grief and pain. Again and again in the past decade we have been touched and wounded by the political process as we had not been wounded before. It is not indifference but the numbness of mourning that lies behind the apparent apathy observers have noticed during the election campaign.

It goes back to President John F. Kennedy whose political and family life were brought extraordinarily close to us on TV. On that terrible day in Dallas nine years ago his death, too, was brought extraordinarily close.

Many Americans simply have not recovered. Even the moguls of TV, men not noted for their sensitivity, seem to recognize this for they seldom show a long film clip of John F. Kennedy in action. They realize that it is still too painful, that the process of mourning is incomplete, that our sorrow is not yet spent.

Not only our apathy, but some of the cynicism the pundits have noticed this year goes back to the murder of J.F.K. For what did his assassination do but stop the political process dead in its tracks, short-circuit democracy by substituting the will of a single madman for that of a nation? Of what value is a system geared to expression of the popular will if the workings of that will can be wiped out in a second?

We still were struggling with our guilt and grief and with political questions raised by the assassination when, five years later, we had to face it again, first with the murder of Dr. Martin Luther King and then that of Robert F. Kennedy. And this year, just as the campaign was warming up, we were reminded of the shock and horror all over again by the nearly fatal shooting of Governor Wallace of Alabama.

Is it any wonder that some of us were tempted to plunge into campaigning this year, tempted to get hopeful about national politics once again, only to draw back out of a dimly perceived need for self-protection? It is not that we have grown morally callous, as the pundits say, or that we have been manipulated into insensibility. It is simply that we want to put some emotional distance between ourselves and the political scene, charged as it now is with feelings of anxiety and pain.

Among politicians, the first to understand was Eugene McCarthy who, even before the murders of 1968, was campaigning with cool and telling us we ought to expect less of the office of President. It was a message we wanted to hear. The fewer of our emotions we invest, after all, the less we stand to be hurt.

But the great beneficiary has been Richard M. Nixon. For some people it is a protection to have a President they do not love or even like. Gary Hart, Senator McGovern's campaign manager, has commented that support for Mr. Nixon is "a mile wide and an inch deep." Exactly. An inch

deep is as deeply as many Americans want to care right now.

We are told that Mr. Nixon needs to pace himself, to conserve his emotional energy and limit his contacts with people. Accordingly, he seldom meets the public face to face and has held far fewer press conferences than any President in modern times. By staying out of sight, by tailoring this aspect of his office to his needs, President Nixon may be meeting our needs as well. His low visibility, which would have been accounted a failure of leadership in other times, may be an accidental stroke of genius for now.

The fact that we have not finished mourning, have not settled our accounts over the deaths of John and Robert Kennedy, has implications for Edward Kennedy as well. Should he run for President he, and we, will have to deal, not with our feelings about him alone, but with the overlay of unresolved emotions about his brothers. This was apparent three years ago when Kennedy drove off a bridge

on Chappaquiddick Island and had trouble accounting for his actions in the hours immediately afterward. The press and public leaped on him. They pronounced him "politically dead." In what they said and the way they said it, there was something savage, something like triumph or relief.

What we were engaged in that year was the symbolic murder of Edward Kennedy. We were killing him ourselves. In that way we could spare ourselves the horror of yet another, real-life Kennedy assassination. By taking matters into our own hands, we were trying, however, to wrest back that control over events that we lost.

It will be hard for Americans to recover. Meanwhile, we are paying the price: the loss of our hope about leadership and a failure to invest the best of our energies and emotions in national politics.

Priscilla McMillan is an Associate of the Russian Research Center, Harvard University.

Read this, please, but don't tell anyone what it says or who wrote it. If you must tell, attribute it to a former Government aide writing in a large metropolitan daily.

By Bill Moyers

Following my address at the University of Maine commencement last June, a student said to me: "Mr. Moyers, you've been in both journalism and Government; that makes everything you say doubly hard to believe." The skepticism which she expressed toward two of our major institutions is widespread, one reason being, I am convinced, the indiscriminate use of backgrounders as the source of "hard" news stories.

The backgrounder permits the press and the Government to sleep together, even to procreate, without getting married or having to accept responsibility for any offspring. It's the public on whose doorstep orphans of deceptive information and misleading allegations are left, while the press and the Government roll their eyes innocently and exclaim: "No mea culpa!"

I know. I used to do a little official seducing myself. The objects of the chase—members of the Washington press corps—were all consenting adults. Having been around much longer than I and being more experienced, they came to each tryst more eagerly than I had expected. As when the noted correspondent of a major network implored me, "If I can't use what you have just told me, can I use what you haven't just told me?" Assuming the classic posture of the incorruptible but ingenuous press secretary—eyebrow arched casually, condescendingly, in the manner of Clark Gable, and a smile like Whistler's Mother—I merely looked him in the eye and he was had. That night his gravelly voice carried to millions of homes across the nation the word we wanted out in the first place but were unwilling to announce explicitly.

Every major newspaper picked up the story the next day, quoting the network reporter quoting "high Administration officials." Never mind that two months later the trial balloon burst. Except for a few crusty veterans in the White House press corps, no one knew who was responsible for the story. And my accomplice? He was back for more. Score one for the Official Version of Reality.

The backgrounder has its defense, most ably put forward, ironically, by the victims themselves, the reporters. Three years ago, in one of those periodic fits of repentance which befalls an ex-press secretary when he has been away from Washington too long, I confessed to misgivings about the practice and suggested some changes. My proposals were modest. Always identify a source by his specific agency, I suggested; this would replace the loose anonymity of "high U. S. officials" with more accountable terms like "a Defense Department spokesman," "a White House source," or "an official of the Interior Department." Embargo the contents of a group background session for at least one hour, I went on, permitting hastily summoned reporters time to cross-check what they have been told. A few other suggestions followed, equally sensible, of course.

You would have thought I had proposed abolishing the First Amendment, so wrathfully did the press corps rise up to proclaim the absolute indispensability of the backgrounder. Perjury, naiveté, and hypocrisy were but the lesser sins of which I stood condemned, perhaps accurately if somewhat excessively. For two weeks one could travel the length of the National Press Club bar by the light of my effigies, no mean distance.

Some of the arguments in support of the backgrounder I appreciate. As Jules Frandsen, veteran head of the Washington bureau of United Press International, wrote: "A lot of skulduggery in Government and in Congress would never come to light if everything had to be attributed." True, but I am not protesting this form of backgrounding. A single reporter digging for a more detailed story can usually check with other sources the information he gets privately from one official, unless he is lazy or on the take. And the good reporters, of which there are many in Washington, learn to throw away self-serving propaganda offered by a disgruntled or ambitious official.

Background sessions which are held to provide reporters with understanding of complicated issues are also useful. Explaining the President's new budget or the ramifications of legislative proposals requires giving reporters access to experts whose names would be meaningless to the public.

But these are not the practices that cause harm and create an unbelieving and untrusting public. It is when the press becomes a transmission belt for official opinions and predictions, indictments and speculation, coming from a host of unidentified spokesmen—when the press permits anonymous officials to announce policy without accountability—that the public throws up its hands in confusion and disgust.

Mr. Kissinger's *sotto voce* threat to the Soviets, which in true Orwellian fashion had to be denied when its source was identified, is only the latest revelation of the ease with which public officials have come to use the backgrounder as a primary instrument of policy, propaganda, and manipulation. "The interests of national security dictate that the lie I am about to tell you not be attributed to me." There are plenty of other examples.

In 1966 an official in Saigon gave a backgrounder in which he led reporters to believe that certain Pentagon studies had forecast a long war in Vietnam—that it would take 750,000 troops in Vietnam to end the war in five years (at the time we had 290,000 men there). The President then told a news conference that Secretary McNamara could find no evidence of any such studies having been made. Later, sources identified only as "U. S. officials" said no such studies had been made, except perhaps as one man's opinion. The source of the original backgrounder turned out to be no less an authority than the Commandant of the Marine Corps, Gen. Wallace M. Greene. Whom was the public to believe: the "high official" in Saigon or "U. S. officials" in Washington? There had been such studies, but the Government, by manipulating the press, obscured the fact.

In 1967 Gen. William C. Westmoreland, the U. S. commander in South Vietnam, told a group of reporters in Washington that he was "deeply concerned" that the Cambodian port of Sihanoukville was about to become an important source of arms for Vietcong troops in South Vietnam. Furthermore, he said, the military was considering contingency plans to quarantine the port. Reporters agreed to hold their stories until the general had left town, and then they quoted "some U. S. officials." The Government was obviously trying to put extra pressure on then-Premier Sihanouk to crack down on the arms shipments—a worthy goal, as the Government saw it. But instead of using available diplomatic channels to reach Sihanouk, Washington enlisted the press as its surrogate. By conspiring to quote plural sources when in fact they had talked to only one man, reporters wittingly became a party to the kind of double-dealing and concealment the press so often condemns on the part of the Government.

Such backgrounders occur frequently. Mr. Kissinger just happened recently to get caught. A mild case of righteous indignation broke out over the incident and some editors have now instructed their reporters to walk out if an official refuses to permit attribution. Representatives of the White House and reporters have been trying to put down some ground rules for the future, but a high source in Washington told me off-the-record that when the rules are issued they will not be for attribution.

In the end very little will change. The Government will go on calling backgrounders as long as the Government wants to put its best face forward. Reporters will be there to report dutifully what isn't officially said by a source that can't be held officially accountable at an event that doesn't officially happen for a public that can't officially be told because it can't officially be trusted to know. But don't quote me on that.

Bill Moyers, press aide to President Johnson and former publisher of Newsday, conducts a regular television program over National Educational Television, Channel 13 in New York.

Politics as Theater of Reality

By Maurice Cranston

LONDON—What is it that people who take up politics actually do? First of all, they talk. For surely if politics is an art, it is one of the performing arts, and not one of the creative ones; Plato noticed this when he compared the politican to the flute player.

But the flute player isn't right either. As a performer, the politican is theatrical, not musical: the world of politics is undoubtedly a stage, and every politican is an actor on it. It seems to me a pity that the word "theatrical" should have become a pejorative one, as it undoubtedly has, and it might be worth pausing to consider why.

The most thoroughgoing attack on the theater that I know of is the one that Rousseau makes in his "Lettre à Monsieur d'Alembert." In this letter, Rousseau depicts the theater as an evil institution with no saving grace or merit, and the métier of the actor as a totally corrupt one. A word that recurs often in this letter is the word "representation." Rousseau attacks the theater because fictions and false-hoods are represented on the stage as realities. In his "Social Contract" he translates this hatred of representation in dramatic art into a hatred of representation in parliamentary government. Readers will remember his argument that representatives or deputies do not, and cannot, represent the people who elect them. As soon as they are elected, Rousseau says, the representatives become the rulers; and the people, instead of ruling themselves, are enslaved by the deputies they have voted for. This is the basis of Rousseau's belief that representative government is fraudulent. Dramatic art he considers an evil for other but equally striking reasons.

About halfway through his "Lettre à Monsieur d'Alembert," Rousseau asks: "What is the talent of an actor?" He answers: "The art of counterfeit: the art of assuming a personality other than his own, of appearing different from what he is, simulating passion while his feelings are cold, of saying something he does not believe just as naturally as if he really believed it."

Politicians, in a sense, do more important work than actors; but why does Rousseau insist so much on the moral distinction between the two? I think perhaps the explanation is that Rousseau had such strong feelings about the disjunction between appearance and reality. He regarded appearance as the domain of deception and therefore as bad; and reality as the province of truth, and therefore as good. The theater was bad because it was an admitted temple of illusions. The political forum, on the other hand, was good, for it was there that men assumed the full reality of citizens. Appearance and reality he conceived to be antithetical; so he could never fully understand the life of politics, where appearance is almost as important as reality: is even indeed a part of it.

Rousseau demanded sincerity, rather as existentialists of more recent times demand authenticity. And this is something far in excess of what we can fairly demand of any political speaker. We expect our orator to be consist-

ent in what he says, to sound as if he believed it, both to be and to appear at least moderately honest. But we do not expect him always to speak as if he were on oath. Franklin Roosevelt was a very worthy statesman, but no one who reads his letters, with their assurances of affection to any Tom, Dick or Harry who might help to get him nominated and elected President, can believe that Roosevelt was literally sincere in what he wrote.

I do not share the view of those who say that Machiavelli introduced the idea of a "politics without morality." His argument, on the contrary, seems to me to be that there is only one true morality: but that the ruler must sometimes disregard it.

It is worth noting that Machiavelli makes no pretense that the bad is anything other than bad. He says that bad things must be done by rulers, but only very sparingly, and then in a manner which is as much concealed as possible. Like Rousseau, Machiavelli dwells on the distinction between appearance and reality. But unlike Rousseau, Machiavelli attaches value to the appearance of virtue as well as to the practice of it. He tells his *principe* that he "should know how to appear compassionate, trustworthy, humane, honest and religious, and actually be so, but yet he should have his mind so trained that when it is necessary he can become the contrary."

We must surely admit that Machiavelli has made an important point here. Since a ruler has to deal with other rulers who are sometimes rapacious and unscrupulous, he cannot easily always observe the same moral law which should govern the conduct of individuals within a civilized community. But at the same time, it is his duty as the head of one such civilized community to uphold the moral law. So even if he has sometimes to contravene the principles of that morality, he cannot let his willingness be known. It is not only that a reputation for deceit makes it hard for a man to deceive successfully. There is another consideration. A *principe* is a prominent person. If he bears visible witness to the notion that deceit is sometimes permissible, other people are only too likely to follow his example in their private lives. And this is something that Machiavelli is most anxious to avoid.

To assert that there are certain exceptions in the application of the moral law is by no means to deny—but rather to affirm—that the moral law has a general application: and a general application so compelling that any exception to it needs careful justification and very delicate concealment. It was certainly no part of Machiavelli's scheme to separate politics from morals, or to contemplate politics in the light of a science from which all normative factors were removed. That was to be the enterprise of a much later generation.

Maurice Cranston is professor of political science at the London School of Economics.

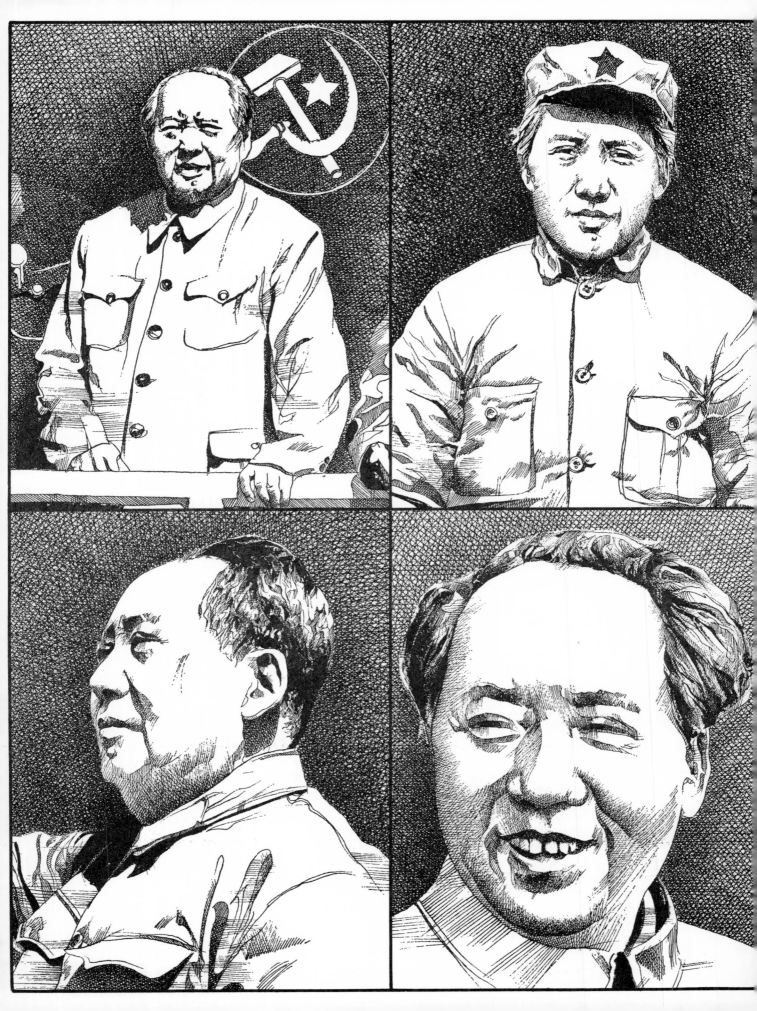

The Return of a Native

By John S. Service

BERKELEY, Calif.—An American returning to China after 26 years comes with different eyes. Absent since before the Communists won the country, he cannot but remember China as it used to be.

That old China was a troubled place—for most Chinese. Warlords, national disunity, civil war, imperialism, unequal treaties, Japanese aggression, ruinous inflation, grinding poverty, natural disasters, callously rapacious rulers.

Since I am the returnee, the reader should be aware of additional frames of reference. I was born in China and, including my youth, spent 28 years there. My personal career as an officer of the American Foreign Service became embroiled in differences of judgment and policies of the United States. My present trip was as a guest of the Chinese Government and based, at least in part, on my friendly acquaintance with many of the Communist leaders during the war years (1941-45) in Chungking and Yenan. So much for background.

For six and a half weeks, from late September to early November, my wife and I traveled some 6,500 miles inside China—north, west, east, and south. One important area we saw—Szechwan Province in the west (and my birthplace)—had long been "off limits" to foreign travelers. I was, in fact, permitted to visit every place I asked to see.

Much of our journey was by air. But the jet age has fortunately not yet reached China. Planes fly low, by day, and preferably only in good weather. The shape of the land, and the mark of man's hand upon it, are plainly to be seen. Even better was a thousand miles by car in the countryside (where I upset protocol by pre-empting the seat beside the driver). In every city we got into the streets, shops, parks, theaters, and restaurants. And, in town or country, I walked—often without guide or escort. My Chinese, though rusty, gave me ears and at least half a mouth; and I could still read.

It is easiest to deal first with the physical changes. In the countryside, the face of the land has been changed by incalculable human toil. Land is saved and gained by elaborate terracing, erosion control, drainage, reclamation. The communes have brought a new layout of the land into larger, more efficient fields. From the air, one sees the neat pattern of the commune members' tiny individual plots clustered close to the villages.

In most areas, graves that once usurped precious tillable land have been removed. This prepared me for finding—when I eventually reached Chungking—that the little foreign cemetery with the grave of my father and elder sister had disappeared. Ancestor worship has disappeared; and so, also, the favored, special status of foreigners.

Everywhere there are irrigation projects: dams, reservoirs, aqueducts, and canals—large and small, completed or still in construction. There have been extensive efforts at reforestation—not all successful. But there are carefully nurtured trees—often in multiple rows—along every road, canal, and railway. In the bleak and treeless landscape of the north, there is a new greenness.

Wherever I went there were telephone and electric power lines. Many communes have their own generating plants. Electricity has brought thousands of pumps for irrigation.

In the cities, there are many new, broad, tree-lined avenues (kept scrupulously swept by multitudes of busy women); some impressive Government buildings (in styles ranging from Soviet to Chinese-palace to eclectic); and a drabness that comes from the absence of colorful old shop signs and advertising (except for political slogans).

In the extensive new suburbs are miles of large, well laid-out factories (often, alas, with smoke-belching chimneys), power plants and refineries, and row upon row of workers' housing.

It is true—though surprising—that there are no derelicts and beggars, no people in rags and tatters, no signs of starvation nor malnutrition. Instead, at street-corner markets in cities such as Peking, cabbages and other vegetables are heaped in great mounds on the ground—and if unsold, are left there undisturbed overnight. Fruit is everywhere in overflowing abundance.

When I was a boy in Chengtu, the rice harvest came once a year at the beginning of September. Revisiting there in mid-October, I was puzzled to find the harvest not yet begun. The answer: the great rice bowl of the rich Chengtu plain has been converted to two-crop rice, each more plentiful than the single crop of the past. Gone are the days when meat was a rarity reserved for New Year and great occasions.

One may miss the brightly gowned upper-class women and entertainers (of various now vanished types) of old Shanghai days; but the people are reasonably well and neatly clothed. Notwithstanding those who have written about the land of "blue ants," there is more color in Chinese clothing now than there used to be. Silk is popular for quilt coverings but a silk brocade factory near Chengtu conceded that some elaborate traditional patterns had not been made since the Cultural Revolution. In Peking (and *not* at one of the special "Friendship Shops" for foreigners), my wife bought an off-the-rack pair of pants of acrylic fiber, handsomely cut, and well made. Her great regret now is that she bought only one pair.

In a commune co-op store (in the countryside near Sian), there was a display of "sanitary paper" (toilet tissue)—coarse by Western standards, but (like bicycles) not an item that farmers had money to buy in the old days.

Were we shown a succession of Potemkin villages? Certainly the Chinese want to make a good impression; we would do the same. But in Szechwan Province and elsewhere, we saw many places never before visited by foreigners (it becomes quite easy to recognize where you are a novelty). And we did not wear blindfolds. One does not need to enter and inspect a commune to be able to see, from the road as one drives past, the number of new dwellings (built and owned by the commune members). In the old days, a new farmhouse was a rarity.

Life is obviously much better for the great majority. There is no longer starvation and bitter poverty. But by American standards, life is still simple, frugal, and austere.

Countries other than China have improved the livelihood of their people. Even Mussolini was able to make the trains run on time. What about the atmosphere and quality of life in China? The answers demand long and intimate immersion in present-day Chinese society—a chance, for instance, to live in a commune for an extended time. These opportunities I did not have. But one becomes aware of a prevailing attitude. Call it, if you prefer, a spirit, mood or temper.

Perhaps the single word that best describes it is egalitarian. It is exemplified, of course, by everyone being a "comrade."

A few other examples: Stopping for tea at a roadside refreshment stand, you invite your driver to join the party. He does so, takes an unselfconscious part in the conversation, and slips away to buy a few persimmons (the first of the new season and not yet sold in the city) to share with all.

My interpreter (a cadre of considerable seniority) engages a gardener at the Ming tombs in a conversation about how the hidden entrance to a recently excavated burial chamber was discovered. The gardener took part in the dig. He talks informatively and with animation. But most interesting to me is the direct, statusless manner in which they speak.

Seeing a harvest crew in the field, we stop the car and walk over. They are operating a new treadle-operated threshing machine. They answer our questions about the machine and the crop. In turn they ask where we are from. But no one is so awed that he stops threshing rice.

In Canton we go to a large garden restaurant. Spurning the special, elaborately decorated section for foreign visitors we join "the people" on the main floor. Our waitress (who has probably seldom waited on foreigners) talks knowingly about the specialties of the house, makes recommendations, answers questions about local matters and rant was crowded to capacity). She asks if we would like a

tour of the establishment and conducts this with aplomb, and knowledgeable pride in the (state-operated) enterprise. (The dinner for five came to $2.20.)

What has produced this new temper? Obviously a great many factors.

China has changed from being a country where the great majority was illiterate to one where the great majority is literate. A half or more of the population has been born in the 22 years since the Communists took power. All children now go to school—most of them to the junior high school level.

Once the ability to read has been acquired, the process of political education can be continued. Our room attendants read "The People's Daily"; and they joined in regular group meetings to read and study the thought of Mao. Most important, with everybody able to read, the historic gulf between the uneducated and the educated, between the peasants and the old literati, has been narrowed—and self-confidence increased.

Another basic change: The status of women. All occupations and professions have been opened to them—with equal pay and such benefits as maternity leave, infant care, and nursery schools. One factory—a shoproom "street industry" turning out small parts for trucks (which are now produced even in Chungking)—was staffed entirely by women.

Gone are the days when women were subordinate, disadvantaged members of society. Shortly before Emperor Haile Selassie of Ethiopia was to arrive in Peking, I left our hotel for a shopping expedition. When I thought to return, it was too late. Traffic control in the areas around the parade route had been taken over by groups of women, mobilized by the street committees and wearing badges to confirm their duties. These sturdy housewives cordoning every avenue were friendly, pleasant, and even sympathetic: but the street was closed and I could not pass.

Another difference is the People's Liberation Army. It has become the paragon of civic virtue and the model of political reliability. Mao himself has summoned the country to "learn from the P.L.A." Its motto, "To Serve the People," has become a national slogan: adopted by every state enterprise—down to the little old lady (with clean white cap and apron, a trim, white-painted pushcart, and a string bag for discarded wrappers) selling popsicles on the Peking streets.

John S. Service was a leading State Department authority on China who was born in China.

Why I Married an American

By Chen Yuanchi

"How did you people meet each other?" "What decided you to marry a foreigner?" I can't remember how many times I ran into these questions when I was an actress with the Shanghai People's Art Theater. Now, just arrived in America, the questions arise again.

My husband, Gerald Tannebaum, is a legendary figure in Shanghai—an American citizen who remained in China after 1949. This inevitably stirred up gossip in Shanghai. Why had he come to China? Why had he stayed on?

I didn't get to know Gerry until 1961. Although I often saw him at the premiere of a new play, we never met. Then at the beginning of 1961 I was given a mission to visit Gerry in his office and ask for advice on a play. It was a sunny winter morning and I was bundled up in my cotton-padded overcoat. His office had a stove which made the room rather warm, so my face was blushing from the heat while we were having our first "business" talk.

My mission was not completed at this meeting because Gerry was being exceptionally helpful and enthusiastic.

"Is he looking for a pretense to see me a few more times?" I asked myself. Strangely enough, our friendship stopped right there.

Several months passed. Unconsciously a bitterness cropped up in my mind. It was my maiden pride—wounded by his negligence. Suddenly one afternoon in June, 1961, I received a telephone call from a man speaking Chinese with a foreign accent. It dawned on me this was Gerry. He told me he was going to come to see our performance that night and would like to meet me after the show.

I said: "Okay."

The first half of the show went smoothly. I was resting in the make-up room during the 15-minute intermission when Gerry strode in. I got so nervous that I pretended he was not looking for me and let my colleagues take care of him. Nobody had any idea that Gerry had come backstage just to look me up.

That night I took my time removing my make-up, hoping to be the last to leave. The head of our troupe had just left before I came out. He had taken it for granted that he was the one being waited for, because usually Gerry offered his opinion after he saw our performances. But to his surprise Gerry made no move, so our director rode away on his bicycle.

Gerry and I went to a nearby coffee shop and had a sundae. People stared, probably shocked to see a Chinese girl accompanying a foreigner alone at that late hour. Gerry walked me home that night. It was quite a long distance, but we didn't notice it. At the gate, Gerry took the initiative. "Why don't we have dinner at my apartment some evening when you don't have to perform?" At first I hesitated, but my curiosity overcame this and I replied: "How about two nights from now?"

That's how the romance started. I must say our theater people were not slow to find out something was going on. The girl who was the head of my study group pulled me aside and asked whether it was true that I had taken a walk with that famous foreigner. I said, "Yes, I did, what about it?" She replied: "Well, there's some talk going on about you and it would be better to watch out."

This was a warning that unless both Gerry and I were serious, we should avoid such gossip because in China if a boy and girl are seen frequently in each other's company, it is taken as a foregone conclusion that they are engaged. Not to carry through to marriage or to break up opens both of them to the criticism of being "irresponsible" or even "promiscuous."

Actually, the gossip didn't bother me too much. I had begun to understand Gerry better and a feeling of admiration emerged. It was the love and faith he had in the Chinese people that moved me. I never imagined a foreigner could be so devoted to another people's cause. As a young man after the end of World War II, he asked to be demobilized from the U.S. Army in China and committed himself to helping Madame Sun Yat-sen in her relief and welfare work, a job which meant neither money nor fame for himself.

As the mystery about Gerry unraveled, a sincere, simple and honest human being came out, true to his own words and loyal to his own belief. The fact that he was an American touched me even more because this gave me, a Chinese citizen, the confidence that real friendship between the peoples of the world is possible.

When a few of my close friends found I was ready to marry him, they became very upset. One girl said: "Do you realize that you are marrying a foreigner whose habits, customs and interests are so different from ours? How can you live together? Besides, how do you know he doesn't have a wife and several children already in the States? What if he should desert you one day?" Others advised me to think twice what kind of consequences this marriage would bring to my political future. Would I be trusted in time of national crisis? All these questions I had taken into consideration.

I believed Gerry would never cheat me, and since he was a true friend of the Chinese people, why should any political crisis between the two governments affect us?

As for my family, I was the youngest of three children. All of us had been brought up by parents who themselves had defied the old custom of arranged marriages. Therefore, we children had been taught to decide things for ourselves. After I introduced Gerry to my mother, she confirmed my judgment in him and nothing more was said. The leadership of my theater took a similar stand. State policy on marriage in China is that there should be free choice on both sides as long as there is no polygamy. So our "widely publicized" marriage took place in 1962.

Years later, in the summer of 1969 during the Cultural Revolution, we held dozens of meetings to summarize, analyze and discuss everybody's history, ideology and problems. This was a sort of ideological house-cleaning. When it came to my turn, I was told by some members of my group that the only question bothering them was why I had married a foreigner. Apparently there were some who questioned the basis and motives of our marriage, who doubted our common point of view and our love. These few wanted to hear another story, one I could not offer.

I was not discouraged by this at all, because through my experience it was obvious that this question persisted only with those who never had personal contact with foreigners, and arose out of sheer fantasy and ignorance. All those who ventured to make friends with Gerry and me eventually overcame their distrust and disapproval.

There is no doubt in my mind that gradually more and more people will understand why I married an American and agree with me that true love and friendship do exist between different peoples.

Chen Yuanchi arrived in the United States as the first un-official Chinese to enter the U.S. from the People's Republic.

Ralph STEADman

The War: The Record and the U.S.

By Maxwell D. Taylor

WASHINGTON—I am grateful to The Times for affording me this opportunity to explain why I think the action of the paper in publishing selected portions of the highly classified Gelb study was contrary to the national interest.

In brief, my position is that this action contributes to further misunderstanding and confusion regarding the events portrayed, tends to impair the working of the foreign policy process, and adds to the disunity which is already undermining our strength as a nation. These views are largely independent of the legal aspects of the case, and of the importance or lack of importance of the classified material which has been revealed.

As history, the articles are unreliable and often misleading because of the incompleteness of the basic source material and the omissions and suppressions resulting from the selective process carried out by the Pentagon authors and the editors of The Times. The Gelb group had only limited access to reports from without the Pentagon, whereas the White House, State, C.I.A., and other agencies were key particpants in the activities under review.

Starting from this incomplete data base, Gelb's analysts exercised a form of censorship in choosing what data to use, or what to exclude. The Times performed a similar function in deciding what to publish from among the 47 Gelb volumes. Thus, in the final publication, the principle served was not the right of the people to know all about the Government's Vietnam policy, but rather the right of The Times to determine what parts the public should know about it. As one member of that public, I would like to know the criteria employed by The Times in making its determinations.

The resulting literary product is a melange of incidents presented in a disjointed way which makes them difficult to understand and to relate to one another. It is hard to distinguish approved governmental actions from individual views of comparatively low-ranking staff officers. There is often a perceptible antiwar bias in the commentary which suggests that the officials involved were up to something sinister and surreptitious rather than carrying out publicly approved national policy. For these reasons, I am afraid that the articles will confuse rather than enlighten the persistent reader willing to wade through them.

The damage which I foresee to foreign policy is from two sources. If it becomes accepted usuage that any disloyal employee of government can find in the press a ready market for governmental secrets, no secret will be safe. In the atmosphere of suspicion and fear of betrayal created within government, one can hardly expect to get forthright opinions and uninhibited recommendations from subordinates who must consider how their views will read in the morning press.

There will be a similar reaction among our international associates. Already we are seeing the embarrassment of allies such as Australia and Canada over references appearing in The Times articles. Other nations are viewing with dismay this latest evidence of internal disarray in the United States and are doubtless reminding themselves of the need for reticence in future dealings with us. Only the propagandists of Hanoi and Moscow find cause for rejoicing. And they are openly enjoying themselves.

My last concern is over the effect of this incident on our national unity, of late a prime target of subversive forces seeking to undermine the sources of our national power. There has been an arrogance in the way The Times has thrown down the gauntlet in challenging the Government's right to identify and protect its secret which assures a bitter public fight. The Times has not only challenged the Government's right to make this determination but has undertaken to substitute its own judgment in deciding what secrets are entitled to protection.

If allowed to continue in its present form, the controversy will provide a further revelation to our enemies of our internal divisions at a time when we need all of our strength and prestige to effect an honorable settlement of the Vietnam war.

There should be ways for reasonable men to reconcile the needs of a free press and of national security without resort to exaggerated classification of documents by the Government or resort to the role of "fence" on the part of the press. Without security a free press cannot long endure, nor can the society and economy which sustain it. Without strong, articulate information media, the Government cannot communicate with the electorate, or win popular support for the needs of national security.

The press should be able to fulfill its secular role of exposing rascals and mistakes in Government without making common cause with the enemies of Government. We must have both a free press and an effective Govern-

ment capable of defending and enhancing our national interests (against all enemies, foreign and domestic). If we expect to remain a great nation, these are not alternatives.

Incidentally, there has been frequent reference of late to the presumed embarrassment caused by The Times articles to the governmental participants mentioned. If anyone is interested, I am not among the embarrassed. In the period covered by these documents, I was working earnestly for peace and security in Southeast Asia, an objective which the Congress had just determined by an overwhelming majority to be vital to the national interest. We toilers in the hot Vietnamese sun took that mandate seriously, and the Gelb study portrays us hard at work in obedience to it.

Gen. Maxwell D. Taylor, retired, served as Ambassador to Vietnam, 1964-1965, and as a special consultant to the President, 1965-69.

The War: The Record and the U.S.

By W. W. Rostow

AUSTIN, Tex.—Mr. Reston's column of June 13, 1971, says this:

"One of the many extraordinary things in this collection is how seldom anybody in the Kennedy or Johnson Administrations ever seems to have questioned the moral basis of the American war effort." He mentions me among others who "concentrated on pragmatic questions ... rather than whether they were justifiable for a great nation fighting for what it proclaimed were moral purposes."

Mr. Reston is quite wrong. The moral and other bases for the position I held—and hold—on American policy in Asia are set out in "The Prospects for Communist China" (1954); "An American Policy in Asia" (1955); "The United States in the World Arena" (1960); as well as in a good many other pieces, including a talk at Fort Bragg in June 1961 and a number of memoranda written as a public servant which have, somehow, not yet found their way into The New York Times. My colleagues can speak for themselves, but I am sure their views were as deeply rooted as mine.

I raise the matter now not in personal defense, for I feel no need for that. I do so because the relation of morality to the national interest has been a peculiarly different problem for Americans (as George Kennan, for example, has lucidly pointed out) and because the question is dangerously bedeviled in current discussions of foreign policy. For reasons that reach back to our birth as a nation, out of the ideas of the Enlightenment, we have tended to oscillate between high-flown moralism and a highly pragmatic pursuit of conventional national interests.

There *are* moral issues involved in supporting the pursuit of the national interest—ours or anyone else's. And they are not simple.

First, and above all, is the question of pacifism. For any reasonably sensitive human being the rejection of pacifism does not come easy. War is ugly and sinful. But pacifism requires an acceptance of all the consequences of never fighting. And this most Americans, including myself, cannot do. That means, however, that all national policy—like the human condition itself—is morally flawed because it envisages war as an ultimate sanction and contingency.

Second is the question of whether the defense of American interests runs with or against the interests of those most directly affected. In Asia this has meant, for example, answering the questions: Did the South Koreans in 1950 and the South Vietnamese in 1961 and in 1965 want to fight for an independent destiny or did they prefer to go with the Communist leadership in Pyongyang and Hanoi? (I can attest that it was this question President Kennedy felt he had to answer above any other before making his critical commitments to South Vietnam in November-December 1961.)

Third is the tactical moral question of conducting war, if it comes, so as to minimize damage to civilian lives. The history of war suggests this is never easy nor wholly successful; but it is clearly a part of the problem and a

legitimate claim on the nation and its armed forces.

Fourth is the broad question of whether the raw power interests of the nation, in general, are decent and morally defensible in at least relative terms. I have for long taken the power interest of the United States to be negative: to prevent the dominance of Europe or Asia by a single potentially hostile power; and to prevent the emplacement of a major power in this hemisphere. These objectives demonstrably accord with the interests of the majority of the peoples and nations of Europe, Asia and Latin America. We could not have conducted our post-1940 foreign policy if this were not so. This convergence of our interests with theirs is reflected in treaties and other agreements which have been approved in accordance with our constitutional arrangements and those of other nations. In the world as it is, I find our power interests, as I would define them, to be morally legitimate.

Fifth is the moral question of the nation's word, once given. For a great nation to make the commitments we have to Southeast Asia involves a moral commitment to stay with them. I believe it immoral to walk away from our treaty commitments, which other nations and human beings have taken as the foundations for their lives in the most literal sense.

I do not detect any thoughtful weighing of these inherently complex moral considerations in Mr. Reston's casual *obiter dicta*. What I do detect is a slipping into *realpolitik* in the next column. What he implies is that, for reasons he does not explain, the fate of South Vietnam ceased at some point to relate to the fate of Southeast Asia as a whole. Mr. Reston appears to have unilaterally repealed the domino theory. As late as 1969, when I last toured Asia, there was great and widespread anxiety from Tokyo to Djakarta about the consequences of premature American withdrawal from the area. And I would guess that anxiety is at least as high today. This is not a moral but a factual question and a matter for judgment on the basis of evidence. We ought to be able to discuss it in a mature and dispassionate way.

In many years of debate about Southeast Asia, I have studied with care and sympathy the views of those who arrived at judgments different from mine. The issues at stake are such that, as Mr. Rusk used to say, they ought to be approached on our knees. My most profound objection to those who would withdraw our commitment to the defense of the area is the sanctimony with which they sometimes clothe their positions.

It is time for all of us to recall these words of Dean Acheson: "On one thing only I feel a measure of assurance—on the rightness of contempt for sanctimonious self-righteousness which, joined with a sly worldliness, beclouds the dangers and opportunities of our time with an unctuous film. For this is the ultimate sin."

W. W. Rostow is former White House adviser to President Johnson.

64

A Soldier Looks Back

By W.C. Westmoreland

WASHINGTON—I will put away my uniform on the first of July, 36 years after pinning on the bars of a second lieutenant. This leads me to reflect, not without some nostalgia, upon the Army I have known and served. In so doing, I find certain constants—truths and principles which have determined the character of the United States Army throughout its proud history. I also find marked evidence of change as the Army responded over the years to the changes in our society and the challenges to our national security. Both—the immutable character, and the change and growth—have opened the way to far greater opportunities for young men entering the Army today than were open to me long ago.

If there was ever doubt, one simple truth has been reaffirmed beyond question during the time I have been a soldier: the United States must have an Army if it is to remain free and great. A healthy skepticism of all things military has been woven into the fabric of our nation since its birth, but no reasoning person can proceed from this skepticism to a conclusion that we do not need armed forces. In a world peopled with imperfect human beings, a world forever in ferment and often threatening, our armed forces are indispensable to our freedom and, indeed, to human progress.

There is another constant etched indelibly in the character of the Army, and that is the code of ethics by which the American soldier lives, works, and fights if need be. The code is best expressed in the credo of West Point: "Duty, Honor, Country." In reflecting on the long reach of American history, I am deeply impressed by the way the Army as a whole has lived up to this code—as an institution, and man by man.

Related to the foregoing, one other constant which I would emphasize is the total loyalty which the American Army has given to the nation and the society it serves. This willing and proper subordination of military force to the leaders, principles and purposes of our civilian society is in itself one of the greatest successes achieved by those who charted our original course nearly 200 years ago.

On the other hand, the Army is a dynamic organization that has changed dramatically during my term of service. Its size has ranged from a Depression level of 165,000 men to a World War II peak of nearly six million. Even at this moment, we are contending once again with the turbulence and manifold difficulties of reducing the Army in size by nearly a half, all the while being required to remain vigilant and competent to carry out our missions.

The changes in Army equipment have been equally striking. The technological revolution has provided materiel far more effective than that with which the Army of the thirties was equipped. The horse and the mule have entered history's stables, to be supplanted by the jeep, the tank and the helicopter. Electronic miracles are commonplace. And of critical importance, the gear of the soldier himself has been markedly improved.

Some other changes come to mind. On a personal note, my monthly base pay as a second lieutenant was $125, which itself was generous indeed compared to the $21 a month paid to a new private. The Depression-era civilian populace, resentful of even the imprudently inadequate military budgets of those days, had little use for the man in uniform and virtually no use for spending money on him. In those days, the very word "soldiering" was a demeaning term implying that someone was slacking on his job. Along with this, troop units were so short of money and equipment that they often were able to do little more than go through the motions of drill without any sense of real purpose of achievement.

Fortunately, for the Army and the nation, there were corps of officers and noncommissioned officers in that long-ago Army who understood why they existed, and who had such a sense of mission that they used the time available to prepare themselves professionally for the challenges which came. They understood—in peacetime—the need for an Army. Since their time, neither the nation nor its armed forces have been free to idle in the backwaters again.

The Army to which young men come in 1972 offers certain enduring opportunities: first of all, the opportunity to belong to an institution which remains essential to our survival and well-being and has as its first mission the preservation of peace through preparedness; and secondly, the opportunity to work at something which puts duty, honor and country above self—a chance to serve other men.

Along with these, there are other circumstances far more attractive than those I remember when I first took my oath. The base pay of a recruit has advanced more than fifteenfold since 1936, with N.C.O. and officer salaries now competitive in most cases with those found in industry. Given the time, the resources and public support, the Army will soon be able to offer young men adequate housing, exceptional training facilities, and almost unparalleled chances for men of all ranks to advance themselves vocationally and academically. Many strides have already been taken in these directions.

There is room within the Army of today for men of many backgrounds, talents, skills and interests. There is equal opportunity to advance on merit. There is interest and meaning in what they do. There are open doors through which they can communicate ideas aimed at improving the Army's effectiveness. And with all this, there remain the mental and physical challenges to the modern soldier.

A look back, then, confirms for me the enduring truths and principles on which the United States Army is based. It reaffirms for me the great pride I have always taken in wearing the khaki and the Army green. It puts in astonishing perspective the strides which have been taken by the Army during my lifetime and the challenging opportunities—personal and professional—which lie before the soldiers of today and tomorrow. If I were able to stand on the Plain at West Point once again and take the same oath, I would do so with equal pride, and even more anticipation.

General W. C. Westmoreland was commander of U.S. forces in Vietnam and Army Chief of Staff.

Just Who Does He Think He Is?

By Gordon A. Craig

At the outset of the Paris Peace Conference of 1919 someone suggested to Woodrow Wilson that he might find it useful to read a handbook, which had been written for the British delegation by C. K. Webster, about the Congress of Vienna and the international system it created. The President flatly refused to do so, with some derogatory remarks about balance-of-power politics and those who had practiced it.

Times have changed. Today we have a President who has expressed the belief that the world will be safer if "we have a strong healthy United States, Europe, Soviet Union, China, Japan, each balancing the other, not playing one against the other, an even balance," and who has as his principal foreign affairs adviser a man who is an expert on the Congress of Vienna and, as his scholarly writings show, an admirer of the most proficient practitioners of balance-of-power politics in the nineteenth century, Metternich and Bismarck.

Does this mean that President Nixon and Mr. Kissinger hope to return to a system like that which obtained in the golden age of classical diplomacy? And if so, is there any real possibility that that hope will be fulfilled?

When it is compared with any of the experiments in international order that have been made since 1918, the nineteenth century diplomatic system seems undeniably attractive. It literally eliminated armed conflict between major powers between 1815 and 1848 and, although shaken by the national wars of the eighteen-fifties and eighteen-sixties, proved sufficiently resilient to shore up the bulwarks of peace for another whole generation. For most of a century, the Great Powers were willing to recognize the legitimacy of the order established at Vienna in 1815 and to seek their objectives within its framework rather than by attempting to overthrow it. In moments of crisis the great orchestrators of the system—Metternich until 1848, Bismarck between 1870 and 1890—were able to alleviate tension by virtuosic performances in the acrobatics of balance, by a wholly unsentimental willingness to adjust their attachments to the requirements of the moment, and by a mastery of the art of defining the context of negotiation in such a way as—to borrow a formulation from Mr. Kissinger's account of the Vienna system—"to make concessions appear not as surrenders but as sacrifices to a common cause."

One may admire all this, but it would be idle to think that it can be repeated. The Metternich-Bismarck system worked as effectively as it did for special reasons. It was ideologically homogeneous; it was severely restricted in membership (until 1890, world politics was largely the preserve of the five major European powers); and, until its last years, it did not have to concern itself with public opinion. International politics was not for the plebs. "The mass of the people," Metternich said with satisfaction, "is always inert." These conditions facilitated the operations of the system and enhanced its chances of success in any given situation. None of them obtains today.

Despite the recent meetings in Peking and Moscow, there is no real evidence, for instance, that either the People's Republic of China or the Soviet Union shares our own interest in creating a viable comity of nations or has any intention of making the kind of agreement about the rules of the game that existed between Metternich and Alexander I or Bismarck and Salisbury. Without such minimal consensus, which might moderate ideological friction, what hope do we have of attaining the "even balance" desired by Mr. Nixon? And even if that balance, by some miracle did materialize, what reason do we have to suppose that it would influence, let alone control, the actions of other members of the diplomatic community, who are much more numerous, in some cases greedier, and generally more resentful of Great Power dominance than lesser powers were in an earlier age? At the very least, persuading others to accept our prescription for a better world promises to be a laborious and protracted business.

And therein may lie the chief difficulty. In an article in the current issue of "Foreign Policy," Stanley Hoffmann has argued that the United States Government today has neither the bureaucratic resources nor the degree of public support necessary to maintain a balance-of-power policy. Mr. Nixon's new policy, he says, "offers a skillful, more modest, more flexible rationale for continuous involvement" in world affairs; but the public mood, after Vietnam, is one of disinvolvement, and this might well be aggravated by a policy of elaborate and ceaseless maneuver which did not yield tangible results. In any case, the concept of balance of power has traditionally had sinister connotations for the average American, and appeals to it are hardly likely to inspire enthusiasm or to reverse tendencies in public opinion (lack of interest in foreign policy among university studies, for example) that are already making it difficult to recruit an adequate pool of gifted foreign-policy personnel.

Mr. Hoffmann actually suggests that this last difficulty has been heightened by Mr. Kissinger's Metternichian star turns on the diplomatic stage, his "grand solo performance" which dazzles but discourages new talent. If there is anything in this, it is ironical, since Mr. Kissinger's final judgment on Bismarck is that he was a failure precisely because he neglected to train an élite to carry on his work. But it seems apparent in any case that the special assistant for national security affairs does not overvalue the manipulative dexterity of the two great diplomatic luminaries of the nineteenth century. From his writings it is clear that what he admires in them is the persistence of their search for a viable international order, and, even here, he is too good a historian to close his eyes to the fact that our similar quest is conditioned by different factors than theirs or to forget that, if diplomacy is the art of the possible, the range of possibility is defined in our times most severely by the domestic support that it can command. For the President and Mr. Kissinger that is a fact of life, as it would be for Senator McGovern if he should be elected in November. And, as Mr. Kissinger says in his essay on Bismarck, quoting the German Chancellor, "Facts cannot be changed; they can only be used."

Gordon A. Craig is J. E. Wallace Sterling Professor of Humanities at Stanford.

METTERNISSINGER

TIM

A Faceless Mass Called Workers

By Milovan Djilas

BELGRADE—Communist ideas did not spring forth from the working class. Doctrinaires and political movements put them there instead. Marx and Lenin were aware of the difference between Communist theory and the working-class movement. The advantage of Marx and Lenin over other theoreticians and Communist leaders is that for them the revolution and the new society provide the link between their "scientific" views and the working class, that is, the labor movement.

According to Marx and Lenin and the Communists, any movement and any class activity not inspired and led by their "science" not only is not revolutionary and not socialist, but logically is not even of the working class. This claim broadened the base of the revolution and, more important, strengthened the convictions of the revolutionaries.

For this reason Communists, despite their best intentions, cannot look upon the working class and its interests and conditions in any other way except in relation to the revolution or—after victory—in relation to power. Depending on the times and the conditions, the influence of Communists over the working class has been stronger or weaker. But a complete linking of Communist ideology with the working class has never occurred. Moreover, as Communist rule continues, that is, as industrialization progresses, the gap between ideology and class increases and ultimately reveals itself to be unbridgeable.

The origin of that difference is to be found in the ideology itself: just as Hegel's Absolute Spirit was destined to prevail in the world, in the same way the "laws of history" destine Marx's proletariat to destroy capitalism and to construct the "perfect"—classless—society. However, the life and the aspirations of the working class, like those of every other social stratum, developed without regard for and even contrary to the "historical mission" which the ideologists and revolutionaries had assigned to the working class.

However, Marx's theories about the working class as gravediggers of the class society and builders of· the classless society are neither superficial nor fantastic.

In Marx's time classes, especially in Britain which he studied the most carefully, were clearly distinct and in opposition to each other. That was the epoch of scientific technology and of the bourgeoisie, but also of bitter class conflict. Here and there in Europe the proletarian masses, exploited and deprived of their rights, burst out in rebellion. There also grew up various philanthropic and reformist doctrines about equality and absolute freedom. Marx, however, understood the inevitability of the industrial

transformation of humanity. And it was only thereby that the working class—the most important human factor of that transformation—acquired crucial social significance. Workers need neither mercy nor understanding: their very role in production makes workers powerful and organized to obtain their rights.

Developments thus far have proved Marx correct in that respect and have affirmed that he is the most profound and far-reaching prophet of modern times. The development of Europe best confirms the validity of Marx's analysis and his specific predictions. In Europe at the end of the nineteenth and the beginning of the twentieth century was to occur a joining together of Communist ideology and labor movements such as was never seen before or since.

But Marx was wrong when he predicted ever greater impoverishment of the working class in industrial countries and, following from that, the inevitability of the proletarian revolution. Revolutions took place not in industrial countries but in countries which were not able to industrialize without first violently destroying the old order. The working class in such countries was too weak; the revolution was mainly the work of professional revolutionaries and of the impoverished and nationally oppressed peasantry (soldiers). Such revolutions were ideologically "proletarian," but not socially.

The greatness of Lenin is that he makes up for the "weakness" and "lack of consciousness" of the class with the avant-garde, the ideological party. In that way he discovered the means to revolution and to new power—means which Marx had conceived but was unable to develop in a liberal and industrial Europe.

The working class accepts the new revolutionary authority and the new property relations since they regulate working conditions and assure basic necessities. But this does not abolish the incompatibility between the working class and the ideological party as the wielder of power. Lenin was to insist upon the initiatory role of the Soviet and upon strengthening the workers within them. But he was quick to free himself from the illusion that a class or a mass can exercise power directly. To take the "leading role" in power and in society, he had at his disposal the party which had carried out the revolution. He was to rely upon it most of all.

The incompatibility between the Communists and the working class is evident in the revolution as well as in the victory: the Communists attack all non-Communist socialist and labor activities as "alien" and thereby separate themselves from the class and set themselves above it.

Manifest
der
Kommunistischen
Partei

Veröffentlicht im Februar 1848.

Proletarier aller
Länder vereinigt euch.

———————————

London,
Gedruckt in der Office der
„Bildungs=Gesellschaft für Arbeiter"
von J. E. Burghard.
46, LIVERPOOL STREET, BISHOPSGATE.

Communists might have hoped that with their coming to power the incompatibilities between them and the working class would cease to exist. For according to Communist theory, power should have been only an organ of the working class against conspiracies and intervention. That organ should immediately begin to wither away and should completely wither away with the construction of the classless, socialist society.

But it is as if Communism had jinxed itself: at the very moment when it appears that Communist predictions and ideals are about to be realized, they turn into their own contradictions.

Thus, when the Communists come to power, the working class and Communism mutually move apart and become estranged. This happens unevenly and in different ways. Viewed in perspective, this coincides with the transformation of the party bureaucracy into a privileged, monopolistic stratum. A special élite is created—a "new class." It justifies its activity as the "continuation of the revolution," but its *raison d'être* is absolute power as the means to industrialization. The revolutionary organs, where the voice of the workers was once heard, retain their form but they are now elected and operate under the direct control of the party apparatus. The working class self-sacrificingly accepts industrialization and spares neither sweat nor blood in fighting the Fascist conquerors: there the interests of the party bureaucracy and the working class coincide.

But this is still the idealistic, heroic phase of Communism. Communists are fighting and dying in the belief that they are the only authentic representatives of the class and its "historic mission." If they die, they are dying for the faith; victory will be theirs alone.

For that reason, the purges hurt the working class less than other strata (peasants, intelligentsia, bourgeoisie). The bureaucracy alienates the working class from politics and transforms it into a faceless labor force without which there can be no industrialization and no industry. Workers are the only stratum which is not "alien" and socially suspect.

Such conditions in fact transform the working class into a mass and destroy the tie between the individual and his social community. The worker is thus only a worker, but not a member of his class—if by class we also mean an expression of group aspirations and interests and not only, as the Communist texts say, a specific role in production. The interests and aspirations of the class exhaust themselves in party resolutions. And how could it be otherwise when already much earlier "class consciousness" has been equated with ideology and the autonomy of the class equated with the activity of party forums?

In truth, that is "society"—at least in Eastern Europe—since the time of the ideological darkness of Stalin. But it is also true that no country in Eastern Europe has yet come to any kind of awareness of the special interests of the working class and even less to an awareness of the autonomy of the working organization.

The least enviable position in that process of subduing the workers and transforming them into a faceless mass was, and still is, held by the trade union. Persons outside of Communism find it difficult to understand why such trade unions exist. In the time of Lenin there was a sharp debate within the Soviet party about the need for trade unions. Lenin's views of trade unions as the "school of Communism" prevailed. But that school did not develop. Stalin transformed the trade unions as well as other nonparty organizations into "transmission belts" for the party center. The real work of trade unions was reduced to increasing production and productivity. Today the parasitic trade-union bureaucracy is barren and absurd. This is most obvious in Yugoslavia, not because trade unions here are more subservient than in other Communist countries. On the contrary, Yugoslav trade unions take more initiative and are more enterprising. The futility of Yugoslav trade unions is only more visible because Yugoslavia has gone the furthest in de-ideologizing and in establishing a market economy.

The nature and methods of Communist power evoke the most profound doubt about Communism as a workers' movement. But even here one should be cautious about categorical conclusions. There is no doubt that Communism is estranged from the working class. But in specific conditions it is capable of linking itself with the most militant parts of that class (for example, in Italy or France) and even of realizing certain interests of the entire class (in reconstruction and industrialization). But Communism is not a workers' movement; like everything else, the working class and its struggles and demands are to the Communists merely means to attaining "higher" ends.

Spellbound by ideology and by power, Communists have never anywhere fully understood the working class. It is, by its nature and role, a creative, nonexclusive class. Marx could conceive a world without the bourgeoisie, and we can even imagine one without the ideological party bureaucracy. But no past or present world is conceivable without the working class.

Milovan Djilas is the Yugoslav revolutionary and Marxist theoretician.

Blue-Collar Revolution

By Herbert Marcuse

SAN DIEGO—The prevalence of a nonrevolutionary—nay, antirevolutionary—consciousness among the majority of the working class is conspicuous.

To be sure, revolutionary consciousness has always expressed itself only in revolutionary situations; the difference is that, now, the condition of the working class in the society at large militates against the development of such a consciousness. The integration of the largest part of the working class into the capitalist society is not a surface phenomenon; it has its roots in the political economy of monopoly capitalism: benefits accorded to the metropolitan working class thanks to surplus profits, neocolonial exploitation, the military budget, and gigantic government subventions. To say that this class has much more to lose than its chains may be a vulgar statement but it is also correct.

It is easy to brush aside the argument of the tendential integration of the working class into advanced capitalist society by stating that this change only refers to the sphere of consumption and thus does not affect the "structural definition" of the proletariat.

The political potential of rising expectations is well known. To exclude the sphere of consumption in its broader social aspects from the structural analysis offends the principle of dialectical materialism. Still, the integration of organized labor is a surface phenomenon in a different sense: it hides the *dis*integrating, centrifugal tendencies of which it is itself an expression. And these centrifugal tendencies do not operate *outside* the integrated domain; in this very domain the monopolistic economy creates conditions and generates needs which threaten to explode the capitalist framework.

I recall the classical statement: it is the overwhelming *wealth* of capitalism which will bring about its collapse. Will the *consumer society* be its last stage, its gravedigger?

There seems to be little evidence for an affirmative answer. At the highest stage of capitalism, the most necessary revolution appears as the most unlikely one.

Most necessary because the established system preserves itself only through the global destruction of resources, of nature, of human life, and the *objective* conditions for making an end to it prevail.

Those conditions are a social wealth sufficient to abolish poverty; the technical know-how to develop the available resources systematically toward this goal; a ruling class which wastes, arrests and annihilates the productive forces; the growth of anticapitalist forces in the Third World, and a vast working class which, separated from the control of the means of production, confronts a small, parasitic ruling class.

But at the same time the rule of capital, extended into all dimensions of work and leisure, controls the underlying population through the goods and services it delivers and through a political, military, and police apparatus of terrifying efficiency. The objective conditions are not translated into a revolutionary consciousness; the vital need for liberation is repressed and remains without power.

The class struggle proceeds in the forms of an "economistic" contest; reforms are not made as steps toward revolution—the subjective factor is lagging behind.

However, it would be wrong to interpret this discrepancy between the necessity and possibility of revolution only in terms of a divergence between the subjective and objective conditions.

The restabilization of capitalism and neoimperialism, which began after the second World War, has not yet come to an end—in spite of Indochina, in spite of inflation, the international monetary crisis, and rising unemployment in the United States. The system is still capable of "managing," by virtue of its economic and military power.

It is precisely the unprecedented capacity of twentieth-century capitalism which will generate the revolution of the twentieth century—a revolution, however, which will have a base, strategy, and direction quite different from its predecessors, especially the Russian Revolution. Its features were the leadership of an "ideologically conscious avant-garde," the mass party as its "instrument," the basic objective the "struggle for the state power."

The mass base created by the relation between capital and labor in the eighteenth and nineteenth centuries no longer exists in the metropoles of monopoly capital, and a new base is in the making, an extension and transformation of the historical one by the dynamic of the mode of production.

At the latest stage of economic and political concentration, ever more strata of the formerly independent middle classes become dependent employes, separated from control of the means of production. The "tertiary sector" (production of services), long since indispensable for the realization and reproduction of capital, recruits a huge army of salaried employes. At the same time, the increasingly technological character of material production draws the functional intelligentsia into this process. The base of exploitation is thus enlarged beyond the factories and shops, and far beyond the blue-collar working class.

Communist strategy has long since acknowledged the decisive changes in the composition of the working class. The following statement is taken from the discussion of the theses for the nineteenth congress of the French Communist party: " ... the Communist party has never confused membership in the working class with manual labor .... With actual progress in technology and the growth in the number of nonmanual workers, it becomes in fact more difficult to separate manual and intellectual labor although, the capitalist mode of production tries to maintain this separation."

Today's working class is greatly enlarged: it is composed "not only of the proletarians in agriculture, in the factories, mines, construction yards who form the core of this class, but also of the sum-total of those workers who intervene directly in the preparation and functioning of the material production." In this transformation of the working class, not only new strata of salaried employes are "integrated" into this class, but also "occupations which were not part of the sector of material production assume a productive character."

The extended scope of exploitation, and the need to integrate into it additional populations at home and abroad, makes for the dominant tendency of monopoly capitalism: to organize the *entire* society in its interest and image.

The process of capital-realization draws ever larger strata of the population into its orbit—it extends beyond the blue-collar working class.

The enlarged universe of exploitation is a totality of machines—human, economic, political, military, educational. It is controlled by a hierarchy of ever more specialized "professional" managers, politicians, generals, devoted to maintaining and enlarging their respective dominion, still competing on a global scale, but all operating in the overriding interest of the capital of the nation as a whole—the nation *as* capital, imperialist capital.

True, this imperialism is different from its predecessors: more is at stake than immediate and particular economic requirements. If the security of the nation now demands military, economic, and "technical" intervention, where indigenous ruling groups are not doing the job of liquidating popular liberation movements, it is because the system is no longer capable of reproducing itself by virtue of its own economic mechanisms.

This task is to be performed by a state which is faced, in the international arena, with a militant opposition "from below" that, in turn, sparks the opposition in the metropoles. And when today the deadly play of power politics leads to an effective cooperation and an effective division of spheres of influence between the state-socialist and state-capitalist orbit, this diplomacy envisages the common threat from below.

But the "below" is, in scope and structure, larger than at preceding stages corresponding to the enlarged base of exploitation.

To sum up: the working class remains the potentially revolutionary class, although it would be a class of different composition and with a different consciousness. In line with the new character of production in advanced monopoly capitalism, it comprises manual and intellectual labor, blue collar and white collar. The impulses for radical change would be rooted, not primarily in material privation but in human degradation (which finds its most brutal expression in the organization of the assembly line), and in the awareness that it can be otherwise, here and now: that technical progress can become human liberation, that the fatal union of growing productivity and growing destruction can be broken. New needs are becoming a material force: the need for self-determination, for a nonrepressive organization of work; the need for a life that has not only to be "earned" but is made an end in itself.

The new radical consciousness is still largely repressed, diffuse; it is articulated mainly among the oppressed racial minorities, among students, women. But it is spreading among labor itself, especially among young workers. The refusal to continue the way it is appears in the high rate of absenteeism, wildcat strikes, individual and group sabotage, and in the radicalization of grievances: the demands not only for the improvement of wages and specific work conditions, but also for a fundamental reorganization of the work itself. The organization of this opposition may well be the next step.

Herbert Marcuse, professor of philosophy at the University of California, is author of "Counterrevolution and Revolt," from which this article is adapted.

They Never Say I

By Richard Sennett and Jonathan Cobb

In a class society, laborers are confronted with the fact that they are treated as a mass, as nobody special, that they are run-of-the-mill Americans. These definitions are the ones that people who do manual work make of themselves. If being nobody special is not awarded much prestige in this society, however, it is a condition which all the nobodies have learned to share. In contrast to the situation for someone closer to the top, a man near the base of the pyramid who gains approval from those above faces a loss of real respect from his peers. Will he be tempted by his success to act as though his peers not so singled out are no longer worthy of him? If he puts on airs, he will lose the friends of a lifetime.

A whole strain of conservative thought from de Tocqueville to Ortega y Gasset argues that the "masses" are intolerant of diversity and individual differences. Yet it is not a question here of mass psychological pressures toward conformity. It is precisely because being nobody carries a certain stigma in this very unequal society that a subtle kind of emotional arrangement has to be made in the life of someone who is just ordinary when he does something to distinguish himself.

"They gave me a pay raise when the south wall mess was straightened out," says a young plumber to explain a feat of re-engineering he did on a construction project with faulty plans. Although obviously quite pleased with what he had done, the plumber could not use "I did" to describe what in fact he did do. Instead, "the south wall mess was straightened out." Similarly, George Corona "was moved" from supervising two men to nine; William O'Malley "was put to work" on the most intricate machine on the line; Frank Rissarro, ill-educated, has been "lucky enough" to hold a demanding white-collar job for several years. In each case the passive voice replaces an "I," an I that would otherwise seem the master of a situation.

The loss of "I" wards off social isolation. If I act as though my "real" self is someone divorced from the person who does well in situations when high authority asks it, if my competence or power to cope is held at arm's length, as though it were a power external to me as a human being, then when I achieve a new position or other reward from a higher power, I can pass it off as something I didn't do.

Advancement through approval, promotion, even such mundane cues as having a superior ask one's opinion or advice, now do not have to get in the way of fraternity with those around me who have not succeeded. I can still be accepted as a friend, as someone who is not deserting them or putting them in a bad light, because "I" really have not done anything to make this change occur. Passivity has a real place in the life of men who want friends, because the institutions in which men pass their days make it so. Fragmenting the social information in one's consciousness is another, closely related, defense against class injuries.

George O'Mora initially appears to the outsider as a man who never makes connections about his experience that the outsider immediately makes. At one point he spoke about his children: "The thing I'm hopeful for is this: they can make whatever they want of themselves. I know I'm never going to stand in their way, I know I'm never going to push them, they're free." Ten minutes later he was talking about how hard it is for young people to do what they want in terms of work no matter how permissive their parents are, social opportunities having, he believes, dried up. This kind of compartmentalizing of attitudes emerges again and again in George O'Mora's talk. Indeed, it characterizes in one way or another almost all the people we interviewed.

One tends to think of fragmentation in a life as the result of some social disorganization in which the person has been ripped apart. Yet listening to George O'Mora talk, or William O'Malley or Frank Rissarro, one feels a great sense of presence and solidity. Given the fact of being nameless in society, given the ambushes and contradictions of dignity that class creates, the more a man's actions are split up in his own mind the less chance he has of being overwhelmed as a whole. Someone like O'Mora is one person in the midst of these contradictions, because he has no desire to connect neatly all the parts of himself.

Fragmentation and divisions in the self are the arrangements consciousness makes in response to an environment where respect is not forthcoming as a matter of course. We think of "alienation" as a disease, but feeling alienated makes these men strong against the injuries of class.

Richard Sennett, associate professor of sociology at New York University, and Jonathan Cobb of the Center for the Study of Public Policy, are co-authors of "The Hidden Injuries of Class."

Art—for Man's Sake

By Aleksandr I. Solzhenitsyn

Like that bewildered savage who picks up a strange and wondrous object . . . perhaps something thrown up by the sea, perhaps disinterred from the sand or dropped from the heavens . . . an object intricate in its convolutions, now shining with a dull glow, now with a bright shaft of light . . . who turns it over and over in his hands, trying to find some way of putting it to use, trying to find in it some humble function and never conceiving of a higher purpose . . .

So likewise we, holding Art in our hands, vaingloriously considering ourselves to be its owner, undertake brazenly to give it direction, to renovate it, to reform it, to issue manifestos about it, to sell it for money. We use it to play up to those who possess power. We employ it at times for amusement—even in music hall songs and night clubs—and at times, grabbing hold of it however we can, for transient and limited political and social needs. But Art is not desecrated by these carryings on. It does not lose sight of its own origins because of them. And each time and in each mode of its use, it sheds on us a portion of its secret inner light.

But can we embrace *all* that light? Who is there so bold as to proclaim that he has defined art? That he has enumerated all its facets? Yet, perhaps it did happen in ages past someone comprehended and gave this its name, but we grew impatient; we listened in passing and paid no heed and discarded it immediately in our eternal haste to replace even the very best with something else just because it is new! And then later when what is old is said again we forget that we have heard it before.

One artist imagines himself the creator of an independent spiritual world and takes on his shoulders the act of creation of that world, of its population, assuming total responsibility for it—but he stumbles and breaks down because there is no mortal genius capable of bearing such a load; just like man who once declared himself the center of all existence and was incapable of creating a balanced spiritual system. And then when failure occurs, it is all blamed on the eternal disharmony of the world, on the complexity of the contemporary shattered soul, or the stupidity of the public.

Another artist realizes that there is a supreme force above him and works gladly away as a small apprentice beneath God's heaven, even though his responsiblity for everything he writes or draws and for the souls which perceive it is all the more severe. But still: it was not he who created this world, nor is it he who provides it with direction, and he has no doubts of its foundations. The artist is only given to sense more keenly than others the harmony of the world and all the beauty and savagery of the human contribution to it—and to communicate this poignantly to people. And even in the midst of failures and down at the very lower depths of existence—in poverty, prison, illness—the sensation of a stable harmony will never leave him.

However, all of the irrationality of art, its blinding twists and turns, its unpredictable discoveries, its soul-shaking impact on people are too magical to be contained within the world-outlook of an artist, by his conception or by the work of his unworthy fingers.

Archaeologists have not yet discovered any stage of human existence without art. Even in the half-light before the dawn of humanity we received this gift from Hands we did not manage to discern. Nor did we manage to ask: why was this gift given us and what are we to do with it?

And all those prophets who are predicting that art is disintegrating, that it has used up all its forms, that it is dying, are mistaken. We are the ones who shall die. And art will remain. And the question is whether before we perish we will understand all its aspects and all its ends.

Not all can be given names. Some of them go beyond words. Art opens even the chilled, darkened heart to high spiritual experience. By the instrumentality of art sometimes we are given—vaguely, briefly—insights which logical processes of thought cannot attain.

Like the tiny mirror of the fairy tale: You look into it and you see—not yourself—but for one fleeting moment the Unattainable to which you cannot leap or fly. And the heart arches . . .

II

Dostoyevsky once let drop the enigmatic phrase: "Beauty will save the world." What does this mean? It seemed to me for a long time that this was a mere phrase. Just how could such a thing be possible? When in our bloodthirsty history had beauty saved someone from anything? Beauty had ennobled us, had lifted our spirits—but whom had it ever saved?

However, there is a special quality in the essence of beauty, a special quality in the status of art: The conviction carried by a genuine work of art is absolutely indisputable and tames even the strongly opposed heart. One can construct a political speech, a journalistic polemic, a social program, a philosophical system, so that it seems smooth, well-structured, and yet it is built upon a mistake, a lie; and what is hidden, what is distorted will not immediately become visible. And an answering speech, or commentary, or program, or a different philosophy can be counterposed to the first—and it, too, will seem well-structured and smooth, and everything will seem to fit. And because of this one has faith in them—yet no faith.

It is in vain to affirm that which the heart does not confirm.

In contrast, a work of art bears within itself its own confirmation: Concepts which are manufactured out of whole cloth or overstrained will not stand the test; one way or another they will fall apart and turn out sickly and pallid and convince no one. Works steeped in truth and presenting it to us vividly alive will grasp us, will attract us to themselves with great power—and no one, ever, even an age later, will presume to negate them. And so perhaps that old trinity of Truth, Good and Beauty is not just the formal outworn formula it used to seem during our heady, materialistic youth. If the very peaks of these three trees join together, as the investigators and explorers used to affirm, and if the too obvious, too straight, branches of Truth and Good are crushed or amputated and cannot reach the light—yet perhaps the whimsical, unpredictable, unexpected branches of Beauty will make their way through and soar up to the very same place and in this way perform the work of all the three.

And in this case was it not a prophecy rather than a slip of the tongue for Dostoyevsky to say that "Beauty will save the world." After all, *he* was given the gift of seeing much, he was extraordinarily illumined.

And, thus, cannot art and literature in actual fact help the world of today?

That little which I have managed to discern over the years I shall try to set forth here today.

III

I have climbed my way up to this lectern from which the Nobel Lecture is read, a lectern not granted to every writer and once only in a lifetime, not just up three or four specially erected steps but hundreds and even thousands of them—unyielding, steep, frozen, out of the dark and the cold where I was fated to survive and where others who possessed perhaps greater talent and were stronger than I, perished. I met only a few among them in the Gulag Archipelago scattered over a widespread multitude of islands. And beneath the millstone of police surveillance and mistrust I did not speak face to face will all those who were there. Of some I only heard at second hand and about others I only guessed. Those who fell into that abyss who already had made a name in literature are at least known to us—but how many whom we do not know, never once were published! And so very few, almost no one, managed to survive and return. A whole national literature remained behind, not only buried without coffins and graves, but also even without underwear, naked, except for an identification tag on the toe. Russian literature never ceased for one moment! Yet from outside it seemed a desert. Where a thick forest might have grown there remained after all the timbering only two or three trees which missed being cut down.

And today, how am I, accompanied as I am by the spirits of those who perished, with my head bowed as I let pass ahead of me up to this lectern others who were worthy of it, how am I supposed to divine and express that which *they* would have wished to say?

This duty has long weighed upon me and I have understood it. In the words of Vladimir Soloviev:

"In chains too we must close that circle
Which the gods have drawn for us."

In exhausting camp marches, in columns of prisoners momentarily illuminated by serried lanterns in the darkness of freezing nights, more than once we felt in our throats what we would have liked to shout out to the whole world if only the world could have heard one from among us. At that time it seemed so very, very clear that all our lucky envoy had to do was to raise an outcry and instantly the whole world would respond. Our entire outlook, both in terms of material objects and emotional actions and reactions, was precisely defined. And we sensed no lack of balance in that indivisible world.

Those thoughts did not come from books and had not been chosen for the sake of harmony and good order: They had been formulated in prison cells and around camp bonfires in conversations with people now dead, hardened and matured in that existence.

When the external pressure lessened, our outlook and my own outlook broadened, and gradually, even if only through a peephole, the "whole world" could be seen and discerned. And surprisingly for us, that "whole world" turned out to be something quite different from what we had expected. It didn't live by what we had expected. It was not going in the direction we had thought. When it came to a swampy bog it exclaimed: "What a divine and lovely meadow!" When it encountered concrete stocks for prisoners' necks it exclaimed: "What a lovely necklace!" And where some wept unquenchable tears, others danced to lighthearted music.

How has this come about? Whence has this abyss arisen? Were we all without feeling? Or was the world unfeeling? Or was it the difference in languages? Why are people not capable of understanding each other's speech? Words resound and flow away like water—without taste, or color, or odor. Without a trace.

To the extent that I have come to understand all this, the content, meaning and tone of my possible speech here, have changed over and over again with the years, that is, the speech that I am delivering today.

And it is by now very little like that which I first conceived on that freezing night in the camp.

IV

From time immemorial man has been structured in such a way that his world outlook, at least when not induced by hypnosis, his motivations and scale of values, his actions and intentions are determined by his own personal and group experience of life. As the Russian proverb says:

"Believe not your own brother—believe instead in your own crooked eye."

This is the most healthy foundation for understanding one's surroundings and one's behavior in them. And through all those long ages when our world was so mysteriously, remotely separated, before it was criss-crossed by lines of communication, before it was transformed into one united and tremulously vibrating lump, people were guided accurately by their own life experience in their own narrow locality, in their own community, their own society, and, in the end, in their own national territory. At that time it was possible for individual human

eyes to perceive and accept a common scale of values: What was considered average, what was considered improbable, what was cruel, what was beyond all bounds of evil, what was honorable, what was deceit. And even though widely scattered peoples lived in different ways, even though their scale of social values might be astonishingly different, just as were their systems of weights and measures, these differences surprised only infrequent travelers, and wound up described in various journals as curiosities which boded no threat for a still un-united humanity.

But then, in our most recent decades, humanity has imperceptibly and suddenly become united—hopefully united and dangerously united. So that a concussion or an infection in one part is almost instantly transmitted to other parts, which sometimes have no immunity at all against it. Humanity has become one—but not as a community or even a nation used to be united in a state of stability: not as a result of gradual life experience, not through the sight of one's own eye which was jocularly called blind, not even through one's own native and comprehensible language—but instead, across all the obstacles and barriers, by the international radio and press. Down upon us rolls a tidal wave of events. Half the world learns in one moment about their appearance, but the standard for measuring these events and evaluating them in accordance with laws of the parts of the world unknown to us is not carried and cannot be carried by the ether or in the newspapers. These standards have been established and accepted for too long and in too special a way in the isolated lives of separate countries and societies. They cannot be communicated instantaneously. And in different regions different, particular, hard-won scales of values are applied—and judgment is delivered uncompromisingly, audaciously, solely on the basis of one's own values and not on that of others.

And though there are not necessarily a multitude of such scales in the world there are at least several: a scale for events close at hand and a scale for events far distant; a scale for old societies and one for the young, one for those well off and another for those which are not. The dividing lines are so startlingly different, so varied in color, that they hurt the eyes, and so as not to feel the pain we brush aside all those values which are not our own as if they were crazy, or would lead us into delusion—and we judge the world self-confidently on the basis of our own household values. And, as a result, the things which seem

to us to be larger, more painful, more insufferable are not those that really are so—but those that are closest to us. Everything which is more distant and does not threaten this very day to roll across the threshold of our home is seen by us with all its moans, stifled screams, destroyed lives—even when millions of victims are involved—as being by and large endurable and within tolerable dimensions.

In one hemisphere, amidst persecutions which yielded nothing to those of ancient Rome, hundreds of thousands of silent unheard Christians sacrificed their lives for their faith in God. And in the other hemisphere a certain madman (no doubt not the only one) dashed across the ocean to free us from religion with a blow of steel directed at the pontiff. On the basis of his values, he arrived at this decision for all of us!

What by one standard seems from a distance to be an enviable and blessed freedom, by another scale close-up is perceived as a vexatious compulsion which stimulates us to overturn buses. What in one region would be dreamed of as a totally improbable prosperity, in another arouses outrage as savage exploitation that calls for an immediate strike. Various values exist for natural catastrophes: A flood which takes two hundred thousand lives seems less important than a local accident. There are different values for personal insults; in some places even an ironic smirk or a gesture of dismissal is a humiliation while in other places cruel beatings are regarded as nothing more than a bad joke. There are different values for punishments and for evil deeds. According to one measure a month of arrest, or of exile to the country, or confinement in a "punishment cell" where the prisoner is fed on white rolls and milk, shake the imagination and flood the newspapers with rage. And by another, prison terms of twenty-five years and punishment cells with icy walls in which prisoners are force to undress to their underwear, and insane asylums for healthy people, and shots fired by border guards into countless unreasonable people who are for some strange reason trying to escape—all these things are quite ordinary and forgivable. And the heart is quite at ease with that exotic land about which in fact nothing at all is really known, from whence no news of any happening reaches our ears, except only the tardy and trivial conjectures of a few correspondents.

And for this dichotomy, for this dumbfounded lack of grasp of someone else's faraway grief, one cannot reproach human eyesight: That is the way man is. But for humanity as a whole, squeezed into one glob, such mutual lack of understanding carries the threat of a quick and stormy death. Given the existence of six, or four, or even two scales of values there can be no one world, no single humanity: We will be torn apart by this difference in rhythm, this difference in oscillation. We will not survive on one earth, just as no man can survive with two hearts.

V

But who is going to coordinate these scales of values and how is it to be done? Who is going to create for all mankind one single system of values for evil deeds and good deeds, for what is intolerable and what is tolerable, and where the boundary between them lies today? Who will make clear for mankind what is really unbearable and heinous and what, because of its nearness to us, is only a scratch on the skin—and, thus, direct our wrath against what is really terrible, and not merely something close to us? Who might be capable of communicating such understanding across the barrier of personal human experience? Who might possibly be able to instill in the narrow, stubborn human essence the grief and joy of others who are far away, a perception of a range of facts and delusions which they have never experienced themselves?

In this, propaganda, coercion and scientific proof are equally powerless. But fortunately the world possesses a means to this end! It is art. It is literature.

A miracle is within its power: to overcome man's liability of learning only by personal experience, unaffected by the experience of others. From man to man, filling up his brief time on earth, art communicates the whole burden of the long life experience of another being with all its hardships, colors, juices, recreating the experience endured by another human in the flesh—permitting it to be absorbed as one's own.

And even more, much more, than this: Whole countries and continents repeat each others' mistakes after a time, as it can happen even now, in an age when, as it would seem, everything is clearly visible! But no: What some peoples have already suffered, considered and rejected, suddenly turns up among others as the very latest word. And here, too: The one and only substitute for experience which we have not ourselves had is art, literature. We have been given a miraculous faculty: Despite the differences of language, customs and social structure we are able to communicate life experience from one whole nation to another, to communicate a difficult national experience many decades long which the second of the two has never experienced. And in the most favorable case this may save a whole nation from a path which is dangerous or mistaken or destructive. And thus the twists and turns of human history are shortened.

I wish today from this Nobel lecture platform to call urgent attention to this great and blessed faculty of art.

There is one other invaluable way in which literature communicates irrefutable and condensed human experience—from generation to generation. Thus, it becomes a living memory of nations. Thus, it keeps warm and preserves within itself its lost history—in a way not subject to distortion or falsification. Thus, literature itself together with language preserves the national soul.

(In recent times it has been fashionable to talk of the leveling of nations, of the disappearance of peoples in the cauldron of contemporary civilization. I don't agree with this, but this is another matter. Here it is merely appropriate to say: the disappearance of nationalities would impoverish us no less than if all people were to become identical, with the same personality and the same face. Nationalities are the wealth of humanity, they are its crystallized personalities; even the smallest among them has its own special colors, hides within itself a particular facet of God's design.)

But woe to that nationality whose literature is cut short by forcible interference. This is no simple violation of "freedom of the press." This is a locking up of the national heart, the amputation of the national memory. The nationality has no memory of its own. It is deprived of its spiritual unity. And even though compatriots apparently speak the same language, suddenly they cease to understand one another. Whole speechless generations are born and die, not telling of themselves either to each other or to their descendants. If such literary geniuses as Akhmatova and Zamyatin were buried alive for their whole lives, condemned right to the grave to create in silence, not hearing a reverberation from what they wrote—this is not only their own personal misfortune but a sorrow to all nationalities, and a danger for all nations.

And in certain cases—for all humanity: that is, when because of such silence the whole of history ceases to be understood.

VI

At various times and in various countries there have been heated, angry, and sophisticated arguments as to whether art and the artist may live for their own sakes or whether they are required always to keep in mind their debt to society and to serve it, even though in an unbiased way. To me this is clear enough, but I am not here going into this argument again. One of the most brilliant statements on this theme was the Nobel lecture of Albert Camus—and I can happily support its reasoning. Yes, and Russian literature has had this same direction for whole decades: not to let itself get lost in self-admiration, not to flit about too carelessly. I am not ashamed of this tradition and shall continue it as best I can. The concept has long been deeply rooted in Russian literature that a writer can do much for his people—and must.

We are not going to flout the right of the artist to express exclusively his own personal experiences and his observations while at the same time paying little heed to everything going on in the rest of the world. We are not going to make a demand of the artist in this respect; instead we will reproach him, ask him, appeal to him and coax him, for this is allowed us. Usually, after all, he develops his talent on his own only in part; for the most part he is endowed with it at birth and along with his talent there exists the responsibility for his free will. Let us grant that the artist owes nobody anything; it is still painful to see how he can, by retreating into a world of his own creation or into the open spaces of subjective caprice, deliver the real world into the hands of mercenary people who are often insignificant or even out of their minds.

Our twentieth century has turned out to be crueler than those that went before it, nor did everything horrible in it come to an end with its first half. Those very same caveman emotions—greed, envy, unrestraint, mutual hatred—which in the course of their flight assumed such high sounding pseudonyms as class, race, mass or trade union struggle, are tearing our world apart and reducing it to chaos. Caveman unwillingness to accept compromises has been elevated into a theoretical principle and is considered to be a virtue of orthodoxy. It requires millions of victims in endless civil wars. It keeps drumming into our hearts that there are no stable and universal concepts of justice and good, that all of them are fluid, that they change, and that this means one must always act as suits one's party. Any professional group, as soon as it finds a convenient moment to grab off something, even if it has not been earned, even if it is not needed, will grab it right away, and society

can go fall apart. The extremes of the up and down oscillations of Western society, as seen from outside, are approaching limits past which the entire system will be unable to return to a state of stability and must fall into ruin. Violence, constantly less restrained by the confines of a legality established over the generations, strides brazenly and victoriously through the world, unconcerned that its sterility has often been manifest and revealed by history. Nor is it merely brute force that triumphs but its trumpeted justification also: the whole world is drenched with the crude conviction that might is right and righteousness nothing. Dostoyevsky's "Devils" who seemed a provincial nightmare of the last century, beneath our very eyes are crawling through the whole world, including countries where they could not even have been imagined; the hijackings of airplanes, seizure of hostages, explosions and conflagrations of recent years signal their determination of shaking and annihilating civilization! And it is quite completely possible that they may succeed. Youth—at an age at when it has no experience other than sexual, when it does not have behind it years of its own suffering and its own comprehension—rapturously repeats our discredited Russian bywords of the nineteenth century while imagining that is has discovered something quite new. The new-found degradation of the Chinese Red Guard movement is accepted by the young in every petty detail as a joyous example. Superficial is their lack of comprehension of the age-old essence of humanity, naive is the faith of their inexperienced hearts: "Now we will overthrow *these* greedy and savage oppressors and rulers, and then we who take over from them, putting aside our grenades and submachine guns, will be just and sensitive." Don't you believe it! And those who have lived their lives and who understand, those who could refute the young, many of them do not dare to refute them, and even flatter them and will do anything so as not to seem to be "conservatives"—and this again is a phenomenon of the Russian nineteenth century. Dostoyevsky called it: "enslavement to progressive fads."

The spirit of Munich has by no means retreated into the past. It was not a brief episode. I would even be so bold as to say that the spirit of Munich dominates the twentieth century. The frightened civilized world found nothing better to counterpose to the sudden return of bare-fanged barbarism than concessions and smiles. The spirit of Munich is an illness of the will of prosperous people. It is the daily state of those who have given themselves over to a thirst for well-being, no matter what, to material prosperity as the principal goal of life on earth. Such people—and there are a multitude of them in the world of today—choose passivity and retreat, anything so that their accustomed life should not be disturbed, anything so as not to have to cross over into hardship today, while tomorrow, they hope, will take care of itself. (But tomorrow never will take care of itself! The retribution for cowardice will only be more cruel. Courage and overcoming arise only when we are willing to accept sacrifices.)

And we are also threatened by destruction because the physically compressed and crowded world is not being permitted to fuse spiritually, because the molecules of knowledge and sympathy are not being allowed to leap freely from one half into the other. This is the ferocious danger of blockage of information flow between the portions of the planet. Contemporary science knows that blockage of information flow leads to entropy and universal destruction. Blockage of information flow renders illusory signatures on international treaties: within a sound-proofed zone any treaty can be reinterpreted at will—or better still, forgotten. It is as if it never existed. (And this is something which Orwell understood very well.) Within the sound-proofed zone the inhabitants are not so much people of the earth as Martian expeditionary forces. They know nothing about the rest of the earth and they are quite ready to trample it down in the sacred conviction that they are "liberating" it.

A quarter century ago the United Nations Organization was born amidst the high hopes of humanity. But alas, in a world without morality it was born without morality. It is not a United Nations Organization but a United Governments' Organization in which governments freely elected are equated with those which have imposed themselves by force, which seized power by force of arms. With self-seeking partiality the majority in U.N.O. concerns itself jealously for the freedom of certain peoples and leaves that of others in a state of neglect. By an obsequious vote it has rejected consideration of private complaints—the groans, the cries, the prayers of isolated little people who are merely people. To such a great organization these are merely insects. The U.N. has never tried to make obligatory for governments as a condition of their membership the best document of its 25 years—the Declaration of Human Rights—and thus, it has consigned the little people to the will of governments they did not elect.

It might seem as if the whole aspect of the contemporary world is in the hands of scientists. All of the technical steps of society are decided by them. It might seem as if the direction the world will take must depend on the worldwide collaboration of scientists, not politicians. All the more when the example of a few individuals shows how much all of them could achieve together. But no, scientists have never made a clear attempt to become an important independent motive force of humanity. In whole congresses they back away from the sufferings of others: It is much more cozy to stay within the bounds of science. That same spirit of Munich has unfolded its enfeebling wings over them.

And what then in this cruel, dynamic, explosive world that stands at the edge of its ten dooms are the place and the role of the writer? We writers do not shoot off any rockets. We do not even push the lowliest of hand carts. We are held in contempt by those who respect only material might. Is it not natural for us also to retreat, to lose faith in the inviolability of good, in the indivisibility of truth, and merely to impart to the world from the sidelines our bitter observations on how hopelessly corrupt is humanity, how degenerate people have become, and how hard it is for delicate and beautiful souls to live among them?

But even this escape does not exist for us. Once having taken up the word it is never again possible to turn away. The writer is no sidelines judge of his compatriots and contemporaries. He is guilty along with them of all the evil committed in his native land or by his people. And if the tanks of his fatherland have shed blood on the asphalt of a foreign capital, the brown stains have for all eternity spattered the writer's face. And if on a fateful night a sleeping trusting Friend has been strangled—the rope leaves black and blue marks on the writer's hands. And if the young fellow citizens of his country impudently proclaim the superiority of debauchery to modest toil, or go in for narcotics, or seize hostages—then all of this evil stink mingles in the breath of the writer.

Shall we find within us the insolence to declare that we are not responsible for the ulcers of the world of today?

VII

However, I am encouraged and emboldened by the vital perception of world literature as the one great heart which beats for the concerns and misfortunes of our world, even though these are represented and visible in different ways in each of its corners.

Beyond the age-old national literatures there existed from early times the concept of world literature—viewed as a network of lines connecting the peaks of national literatures, and as the totality of literary influences. But there used to be a delay in time: readers and writers learned of writers in other languages only after delays sometimes of ages, so that mutual influence was tardy, and world literature as a network connecting national literary peaks did not reach contemporaries but their descendants only.

But today there is a mutual reaction between writers of one country and the readers and writers of another which if not immediate is at least close to it. I have felt it myself. My books, as yet unpublished in my own country, notwithstanding hasty and often poor translations, swiftly found themselves a responsive world readership. Even such outstanding Western writers as Heinrich Böll undertook the critical analysis of them. And through all these last years, when my work and my freedom never quite broke down, when they remained suspended in air in violation of the laws of gravity, seemingly on nothing at all—on invisible, mute public sympathy, I learned with grateful warmth, quite unexpectedly, of the support of the world brotherhood of writers. I was astounded when on the day of my 50th birthday I received greetings from well-known European writers. No pressure brought on me went unnoticed any longer. In that day, so dangerous for me, of my expulsion from the writers' union, a wall of defense was erected by the outstanding writers of the world which saved me from worse persecutions, and Norwegian writers and artists hospitably readied a shelter for me in event of the expulsion from my motherland which threatened me. And then, in the end, my nomination for the Nobel Prize itself was initiated not in the country which I live and write—but by Francois Mauriac and his colleagues. And more than this, national writers' organizations expressed their unanimous support for me.

And this was how I myself perceived and felt that world literature was not an abstraction, not something which had not yet crystallized, something created by the scholars of literature, but possessed a certain common body and common spirit, a living unity of the heart, which reflected the growing spiritual unity of humanity. And state boundaries are still being reddened by blood and heated by high tension wires and by bursts of fire from automatic weapons, and certain ministries of internal affairs still imagine that literature too is an "internal affair" of the countries at their disposition, and newspaper headlines still read: "They do not have the right to interfere in our internal affairs!" And, meanwhile, no such thing as internal affairs remains on our earth. And the only salvation of humanity lies in everyone concerning himself with everything everywhere: the peoples of the East cannot be totally indifferent to what takes place in the West; and the peoples of the West cannot be totally indifferent to what takes place in the East. And literature, one of the most delicate and responsive instruments of human existence, has been the first to take hold of, to assimilate, to seize upon this feeling of the growing unity of humanity. And so I am appealing to world literature today with conviction—to hundreds of friends whom I have never met face to face and whom I perhaps never will see.

Friends! If we are worth anything, let us try to help. In our own countries, torn asunder by the discord of parties, movements, castes, and groups, who is it who has from the earliest ages been a force not for disunity but for unity? This in essence is the position of writers: the spokesman for their national language—the principal tie binding together a nation, binding together the very earth occupied by a people, and in fortunate cases also the national soul.

I think that world literature has it within its power in these frightening hours to help humanity know itself truly despite what prejudiced people and parties are attempting to instill; to communicate the condensed experience of one region to another in such a way that we will cease to be split apart and our eyes will no longer be dazzled, so that the units of measurement on our scale of values will correspond to one another, and some peoples may come to know the true history of others accurately and concisely and with that force of perception and painful sensation they will feel that they have experienced it themselves—and by this token be guarded against subsequently repeating the same errors. And at the same time we ourselves can perhaps develop within ourselves a world view: seeing with the center of the eye, like every human being, what is close, and with the edges of the eye absorbing what is happening in the rest of the world. And so we can create and observe worldwide standards.

And who, if not writers, are to express condemnation not only of their own unsuccessful rulers (and in some countries this is the easiest way of all to earn a living and everyone except those who are too lazy is occupied with it) but also of their own society whether it be its cowardly humiliation or its complacent weakness, or of the feather-brained escapades of youth, or of young pirates brandishing knives?

And people will ask us what literature can do in the face of the pitiless assault of open violence? Well, let us not forget that violence does not have its own separate existence and is in fact incapable of having it: it is invariably interwoven with the lie. They have the closest of kinship, the most profound natural tie: violence has nothing with which to cover itself up except the lie, and the lie has nothing to stand on but violence. Everyone who has once proclaimed violence as his method, must inexorably select the lie as his principle. At its birth violence acts openly and even takes pride in itself. But as soon as it is reenforced and strengthened it begins to sense the rarified atmosphere around it, and it cannot go on existing except by befogging itself with lies, cloaking itself in hypocritical words. It does not always nor invariably choke its victims, more often it demands of them only that they take the oath of the lie, only that they participate in the lie.

And simple is the act of an ordinary courageous human being of not participating in the lie, not supporting false actions! "So be it that *this* takes place in the world, even reigns in the world—but not be with my complicity." Writers and artists have a greater opportunity: to conquer the lie! In battle with the lie, art has always been victorious, always wins out, visibly, incontrovertibly for all! The lie can stand against much in the world—but not against art.

And so soon as the lie is dispersed the repulsive nakedness of violence is exposed, and violence will collapse in feebleness.

And that is why, I think, my friends, that we are capable of helping the world in its white hot hour of trial. We must not reconcile ourselves to defenselessness, we must not sink into a feckless life—but go out into battle.

In the Russian language there are some favorite accumulated proverbs on truth. They express firmly the folk experience, and sometimes are quite surprising:

One word of truth outweighs the whole world.

So it is that on so seemingly fantastic a violation of the law of the conservation of energy and mass my own activity is founded, as is my appeal to the writers of the whole world.

This is the Nobel Lecture written, but never delivered, by the 1970 Nobel Prize winner in Literature, Aleksandr I. Solzhenitsyn of the Soviet Union. Mr. Solzhenitsyn's latest work is "August 1914."

Two Poems by Yevtushenko

My Peruvian Girl

At the hour when newspapers die
  to become nocturnal refuse
At the hour when the dog with biscuit crumbs in his teeth
  stops and suspiciously watches each of my steps.
At the hour, when all base instincts surface,
  instincts hidden hypocritically during the day,
  at the hour when cab drivers shout at me "hey, gringo!"
  "Want a little Peruvian? She's a hot chocolate!"
At the hour, when the post office no longer functions,
  and not only the telegraph sleeps,
  at the hour, when a peasant, wrapped in his poncho,
  slumbers, pressed against the statue of a hero
  unknown to him.
At the hour, when the whores and the muses
  take off the make up from their faces,
  at the hour, when the refuse of the future is
  set into bold headlines across the front pages.
At the hour, when all is visible and invisible,
I walk neither to somebody's house nor from somebody's
  house.
I walk, tired, lonely, like a stray dog
  I walk along Lima's nocturnal avenues,
  resembling the cemeteries of the movies.
The street is awash with spittle and orange peels.
The street smells like the latrine of a giant stadium.
But stop, and look: a human form
  takes shape under a pile of dead newspapers.
Over there, in a mute huddle,
  blaming no one for nothing,
  an old woman made herself a poncho,
  a poncho woven from the sensations of yesterday.
The woman covered herself to hide from the cold,
  she covered herself with ultra-rightism and ultra-leftism
  up to her eyebrows.
Ultra-rightism or ultra-leftism—it's the same for the old
  woman.
The only thing important for her is to feel less cold.
The old woman wrapped herself in scandals and intrigues,
  in the bribes of soccer teams that reach to the ground.
Underneath the celebrated legs of Twiggy, the English
  model,

protrude her bare feet.
Luxury automobiles, submarines, rockets
  weigh her down, pressing her to the asphalt.
Horse races, yachts, stripteasers, banquets,over-
  whelm the shoulders of the peasant woman.
On her back—Hunt, Rockefeller, Onassis, du Pont
  slurp cocktails with bovine smiles.
On her chilled body Mao and Nixon politely play ping-
  pong.
And the white llama in the shop window throws her
  a doleful look through the glass
  as if on the spine of this old woman, through a
  photograph,
  is gathered the steaming blood of Vietnam.
Beneath the refuse of the shameless world marketplace,
  without strength to understand this whole mess,
  it looks, like a persecuted llama—the ancient Inca—
  the suffering mother of humanity.
She is doubled up by the weight of falsehoods.
She is oppressed by the violent tattoo of the headlines,
  but she resembles a living sculpture—
  the sculpture of world truth, beneath heaps of lies.
Oh, llama of the show window,
  press yourself to her tired breast,
  free her from under this guilded crap
  and take her with you to the Sierra Negra.
I, the representative of a powerful State,
  silently bow my head, like a lost child,
  confronted by this suffering face,
  this face of copper crossed with gnarled folds like
  creeks.
Within this woman is savagely hidden,
  is hidden and breathing secretly,
  the most powerful State of the whole world,
  the human soul.
"Do you want a little Peruvian, hey, gringo?" they again
  shout with a whistle.
But I am immobile, I cannot move.
I cannot tell the cab drivers,
That I have found my Peruvian. My Peruvian girl.

The Keys of the Comandante

Our horses are walking to la Higuera*
To the left—the abyss,
    to the right—the abyss.
To think of you, Major,
    is not a heavy load.
Within me is a silent ache,
    resembling the earthquake.
I am filled with the creeks,
    of severe, hard rocks.
My nerves are tense
    as the bridle of a cowhand.
The rhythm of this poem
    is dictated by horseshoes,
stumbling against the stones
    of this deadly path.
For guerrilleros
    around here there are no
    monuments.
Their monuments—rocks,
    with sad, human faces.
The clouds are motionless,
    like thoughts,
like thoughts
    of the Bolivian mountains.
Comandante your precious name
    they wish to sell so cheaply.
With your name industry wants to buy
    new customers.
Comandante! in Paris I saw your
    portrait on little pants called
    "hot."
Your pictures, Che,
    are printed on shirts
You plunged into the fire.
    They want to turn you into
    smoke.
But you fell,
    riddled by bullets,
    by poisonous smiles
not to become later
    merchandise for the consumer
    society.
"Where is the key
    to the school?"

The peasants give me no answer.
    I feel the smell of death.
The wall is white
    like the candle
of the boat
    left abandoned to its fate.
The silence is total.
    Only the buzzard flies.
Horse dung—the posthumous
chrysanthemums.
"Where is the key
    to the school?"
The peasants answer:
    "We don't know, sir,
    we don't know . . . "
Where is the key
    to the case of Che Guevara?
Where is the key
    to the future?
Fear of not finding it,
    panic grips me,
but the key is in our hands—
    of that I am certain
Boys: to shout promises
    and not to fulfill them,
    that's crap!
Our own stumbling has deceived the others.
To the left, boys,
    always to the left,
but not beyond the left
    of your own heart.
Comandante, your hands were severed
    in the square of Valle Grande,
Comandante, over your death
    the wild flowers and guitars
    sing
But,
    The young do not surrender,
    the young, forward!
Ours are the hands of Che,
    they cannot be cut!

The village where Che Guevara was killed.

Yevgeny Yevtushenko is a Soviet poet.

The Sakharov Memorandum
By Andrei Sakharov

I consider it imperative to request that the following suggestions be considered by the competent authorities.

• In my view, the time was ripe long ago for dealing with the question of a general amnesty to political prisoners; including persons convicted by reason of their religion, persons confined to psychiatric institutions, persons convicted of attempting to cross the border, political prisoners given additional sentences for attempting to escape from a camp, or of spreading propaganda in a camp. It is essential to take steps to insure extensive, factual publicity of the proceedings in all trials, especially those of a political nature.

I consider psychiatric punishment for reasons of a political, ideological or religious nature intolerable. It is essential to pass a law defending the rights of persons subjected to forced psychiatric hospitalization; also, to adopt resolutions and the necessary legislative refinements for the defense of the rights of persons presumed to be mentally disturbed in connection with prosecutions on political charges.

• Concerning open public disclosure, free exchange of information and freedom of conviction, it is essential that a draft law concerning the press and other means of mass communication be submitted for consideration by the general public.

• Concerning nationality problems and the problem of departure from our country, it is essential to pass resolutions and laws fully restoring the rights of the peoples resettled under Stalin and to pass laws ensuring the free and unimpeded exercise by citizens of their right to leave the country and to return to it freely.

• Concerning international problems, it is essential to take the initiative and announce (or confirm—unilaterally, to start with) our refusal to be the first to employ weapons of mass destruction (nuclear, chemical, bacteriological or incendiary). It is essential to permit inspection teams on our territory for effective control of disarmament.

It is essential to alter our political position in the Middle East and in Vietnam, vigorously striving—through the United Nations and diplomatic channels—for the earliest possible peaceful settlement under conditions of a compromise.

It is essential to work out a clear and consistent program for further democratization and liberalization and to take a number of steps which are top priority and not to be postponed. This must be done in the interest of economic and technological progress; in the interest of gradually overcoming our backwardness in comparison with the advanced capitalist countries and our isolation from them; in the interest of the well-being of wide sections of the population; in the interest of the internal stability and the external security of our country. The development of our country is proceeding under conditions of considerable difficulties in our relations with China. We are faced with serious internal problems in the areas of economics and the well-being of the population, economic and technological progress, culture and ideology.

The following problems should be noted: aggravation of the nationality problem; complications in relations between the party-government apparatus and the intelligentsia, and in their relations with the basic mass of workers who find themselves in a relatively poorer position as far as living standards and economic situation go and in relation to job promotion and cultural growth, and who experience in a number of cases a feeling of disenchantment with "big talk" and the privileged group of "bosses," a group which for the most part often includes the intelligentsia in the eyes of the more backward strata of workers because of their traditional prejudices.

The state sets as its fundamental goal the protection and the guarantee of the basic rights of its citizens. The defense of the rights of man is the highest of all goals. All acts of governmental institutions are wholly based on laws which are stable and known to the citizenry. Observance of the laws is obligatory for all citizens, institutions and organizations.

Open publicity facilitates public control of the legality, equity and effectiveness of the system as a whole, favors the scientific democratic character of the administrative system, and contributes to the progress, well-being and security of the country.

The nation's basic energy is directed toward harmonious internal development with effective utilization of labor and natural resources. This is the foundation of its strength and prosperity.

Messianism is foreign to this society, as are delusions about the uniqueness and exclusive virtues of its own system and the negation of the system of others.

The basic problem in foreign policy is that of relations with China. While offering the Chinese people the option of economic, technical and cultural aid, fraternal cooperation and joint movement along the democratic path—always keeping open the possibility for the development of relations in that direction—it is essential at the same time to show special concern for insuring the security of our country, to avoid all other possible foreign and domestic entanglements, and to carry out our own plans for the development of Siberia, taking the above-mentioned factor into account.

It is essential to strive for nonintervention in the internal affairs of other Socialist states and for mutual economic assistance.

It is essential to take the initiative in creating (within the framework of the U.N.?) a new international consultative agency—an international council of experts on problems of peace, disarmament, economic aid to needy countries, on the defense of the rights of man, and on the protection of the natural environment—staffed by highly qualified and disinterested persons.

In the area of personnel cadres and administration, it is essential to make decisions requiring greater public disclosure on the work of governmental agencies at all levels, within the limits allowed by the national interest. Matters of special importance include review of the tradition of dealing with problems of personnel policy behind closed doors; extension of open and effective public verification of the selection of cadres and extension of the electivity and actual removal from office in cases of incompetence of managers at all levels. I also have in mind the usual demand in democratic programs for the elimination of the system of elections where the number of candidates does not exceed the number of posts, i.e., the elimination of "elections without choice."

Measures should be taken to facilitate an expansion of agricultural production on the personal plots of kolkhoz farmers, workers on sovkhozes, and individual peasants; revision of the tax policy, expansion of the tracts of land in this sector, revision of the system for provision to this sector of modern and specially designed agricultural equipment and fertilizers.

Finally, we should expand the possibilities and advantages for private initiative in the sphere of services, health care, retail trade and education.

The question of the gradual abolition of the passport system must be examined, since it is a great hindrance to the development of the country's productive forces and a violation of the rights of citizens—especially the inhabitants of rural areas.

In the sphere of information exchange, culture, science, and freedom of convictions, it is essential to encourage freedom of convictions, the spirit of inquiry, and concern for effectiveness. It is essential to discontinue the jamming of foreign radio transmissions, expand imports of foreign literature, join the international system for protecting authors' copyrights, and facilitate international tourism—in order to overcome the isolation which is ruinous to our development.

It is essential to make decisions ensuring the actual separation of church from state, and actual (i.e., guaranteed juridically, materially, and administratively) freedom of conscience and worship.

It is essential to take another look at those aspects of the relations between the governmental-party apparatus and art, literature, the theater, and educational agencies, which act to the detriment of the development of culture in our country.

In the social sphere, it is essential to examine the question of the feasibility of abolishing capital punishment.

It is essential to consider the feasibility of establishing a public watchdog agency which would have the goal of ruling out the possibility of the use of physical force (beating, exposure to hunger and cold) on persons detained, arrested, under investigation, or convicted.

There must be radical improvement in the quality of education.

More extensive measures must be taken in combating alcoholism.

It is essential to step up measures in the fight against noise and the poisoning of the air and water; in the fight against erosion, the salination of the soil, and its poisoning by chemicals.

Concerning reform of the system of health care we must: expand the network of polyclinics and hospitals requiring payment of fees; increase the role of physicians, registered nurses, and practical nurses in private practice; increase the wages of medical workers at all levels; reform the pharmaceutical industry; increase the general availability of modern medication and remedies; introduce closed-circuit X-ray television installations.

In the sphere of law it is essential to eliminate overt and covert forms of discrimination for one's convictions and for characteristics of nationality.

It is essential to consider the question of the ratification, by the Supreme Soviet U.S.S.R., of the Covenant on Human Rights adopted by the 21st Session of the U.N. General Assembly, and of adhering to the optional protocol to that declaration.

In the sphere of relations with national republics, our country has proclaimed the right of nations to self-determination, up to and including secession.

The right of the union republics to secede is proclaimed by the Constitution of the U.S.S.R. In fact, the mere discussion of such questions often provokes prosecution. In my opinion, a juridical analysis of the problem and the passing of law guaranteeing the right to secede would have great domestic and international significance as a confirmation of the anti-imperialist and antichauvinist nature of our policy. It seems quite plain that none of the secessionist tendencies in any republic of the U.S.S.R. has a mass character and that they will undoubtedly weaken in time, as a result of the further democratization of the U.S.S.R.

On the other hand, it is quite certain that any republic which, for whatever reasons, secedes from the U.S.S.R. by peaceful constitutional means will fully preserve its ties with the socialist commonwealth of nations. In such a case, the economic interests and defense capacity of the socialist camp would not suffer, since the cooperation of socialist nations is of a very complete and all-embracing character and will undoubtedly be intensified even further under conditions of mutual nonintervention by the socialist states in each others internal affairs. For these reasons, consideration of this question does not strike me as hazardous.

If, at one point or another, the presentation of this memorandum is unnecessarily categorical in character, it is because of the demands of brevity.

The problems facing our country are intimately related to certain aspects of the worldwide crisis of the 20th century: the crisis in international security, the loss of stability in social development, the ideological dead-end and disenchantment with the ideals of the recent past, nationalism, the danger of dehumanization. By virtue of our country's special position in the world, a constructive solution of our problems—a solution at once cautious, flexible, and decisive—would be of great significance for all mankind.

Signature, A. SAKHAROV
5 March, 1971

This "memorandum" was sent to the General Secretary of the Central Committee of the Communist Party on March 5, 1971. It has remained unanswered. I do not consider it my right to postpone its publication. This postscript is written in June 1972.

As before I cannot help but value the great salutary changes (social, cultural, economic), which have taken place in our country over the last fifty years, taking into account, however, the fact that similar changes have taken place in many countries, and that they reflect a development of worldwide progress.

Our society is infected with apathy, hypocrisy, narrow-minded egotism, hidden cruelty. The majority of the representatives of its highest stratum—the party and government administrative apparatus, the most successful strata of the intelligentsia—hang on tenaciously to their open and secret privileges and are deeply indifferent to violations of human rights, to the interests of progress, to the security of future mankind. Others, in the depths of their souls, are concerned, but cannot allow themselves the slightest free thinking and are doomed to tortuous conflict within themselves.

For the spiritual recovery of the country those conditions must be eliminated which push people toward hypoc-risy and accommodation, which create in them a feeling of helplessness, dissatisfaction and disenchantment. Complete ideological freedom is essential, a complete end to all forms of persecution for convictions.

With hurt and alarm I am forced to note, in the wake of illusory liberalism, the growth of restrictions on ideological freedom, of striving to suppress information not controlled by the government, of persecution for political and ideological reasons, of an intentional exacerbation of national problems.

The wave of political arrests in the first months of 1972 are particularly alarming. In the Ukraine numerous arrests took place. Arrests took place as well in Moscow, in Leningrad and in other regions of the country. Public attention in those months was drawn to the trials of Bukovsky in Moscow, Strokatova in Odessa, and others.

The use of psychiatry for political purposes is extraordinarily dangerous in its consequences for society and completely intolerable. Numerous protests and statements on this question are known.

The persecution and destruction of religion has been conducted with persistence and cruelty over the course of decades—doubtless one of the most serious in its consequences for the violations of human rights in our country.

I write this postscript soon after the signing of important agreements on the limitation of ABM and strategic rockets. One wants to believe in a feeling of responsibility before mankind on the part of the political rulers and officials of the military-industrial complexes of the United States and the U.S.S.R. One wants to believe that these agreements have not only a symbolic meaning, but will also lead to a real lessening in the arms race and to further steps which will soften the political climate in a world worn out with suffering.

In conclusion I think it essential to stress the importance which I attach to the proposal on organization of an international consultative organ of the international council of experts with the right to make recommendations whose consideration would be obligatory for the national governments. I consider that proposal to be realistic, on condition that it receive the broad international support which I am requesting.

I appeal not only to Soviet, but also to foreign readers, hoping for their active help in the struggle for human rights. I hope also that my voice from "inside" the socialist world will in some measure improve comprehension of the historical experience of the last few decades.

Andrei D. Sakharov, Soviet Academician and a member of the Committee of the Rights of Man, wrote this "Memorandum" in March, 1971, to Leonid I. Brezhnev. It is presented here in excerpted form.

Echoes of Pushkin Square

By Valery N. Chalidze

On Dec. 5, 1965—Soviet Constitution Day—a small group of intellectuals assembled in Moscow's Pushkin Square, displaying the slogans "Respect the Constitution . . . " and "We demand *glasnost* (public disclosure) for the trial of Sinyavsky and Daniel!"

Every year since then people have gathered on this day in Pushkin Square to commemorate those in confinement for speaking out in defense of human rights. Fewer and fewer people appear because many have been subjected to repressions, and now the question has become especially acute: will the movement in defense of human rights live on, or will the participants in this movement be imprisoned, exiled, intimidated, broken?

Political repression, so terrible and widespread until 1953, was never completely discontinued in the U.S.S.R. Now it has intensified in comparison with the recent past and become harsher—three years of imprisonment is already considered a mild punishment. (I note here that Bukovsky was sentenced to seven years of confinement and five years of banishment). The intensification of repression and the related decrease in active efforts to defend human rights can also lead to qualitative changes in the character of political trials in the U.S.S.R.

For as long as nine months an arrested person can remain under investigation—up to nine months of complete isolation usually without visitors, without legal consultation and without mail; during this time an experienced interrogator can sometimes extract even from a person who is usually brave and steadfast, a confession of guilt, some expression of repentance and testimony useful for the investigation. There is reason to fear that trials where the defendant confesses will become more frequent. And then, perhaps, the principle of open trials will "triumph" at last: defendants will be so in tune with their prosecutors that it will become possible to publish verbatim records of trials as in the thirties (for example, the Buhkarin trial).

But the intelligentsia did not call for this kind of "observance" of the principle of *glasnost* in Pushkin Square seven years ago. It is not surprising that they stressed this particular constitutional guarantee, for it is well known that a just cause does not fear publicity; ordinary people, and the authorities as well, hide only what is shameful and evil.

But perhaps my pessimistic thoughts are groundless? Perhaps improvement of the international situation will lead to a slackening of repression and a release of prisoners? Many hope this. Many always hope for this.

Recently about forty prominent Soviet intellectuals petitioned the authorities to amnesty many political prisoners. I do not know whether this petition will help, but I do know that silence will not help to alleviate anyone's suffering, and that is why I believe that liberal intellectuals in the West will support this petition of Soviet intellectuals. And, as always, I hope that the authorities will adopt a realistic position and will grant freedom, or at least the freedom to leave the country, to those who, for political reasons, have been sentenced for actions which are not criminal according to generally accepted principles of law. But while victims suffer confinement, let them at least be remembered—those now in psychiatric hospitals—Grigorenko, Fainberg, Borisov, Gershuni and others. And those now in prisons, labor camps or exile, among them such well known protestors as Shikhanovich, Bukovsky, Krasin, Yakir, Lyubarsky, Krasnov-Levitin, Emelkina, Veil and Pimenov.

Hopes that the authorities will adopt a more realistic position with respect to the problem of political repression may be well-founded, for recently the authorities have displayed a certain measure of realism in their handing of such problems as the repatriation of Jews and Germans. Regrettably, success in securing freedom to leave the country has so far been limited to such special cases, but it is important to note that this freedom, as well as the right to return to his country, is a fundamental right of man; the protection of freedom of movement plays an important role in promoting the free exchange of information and the growth of legal consciousness among people. And, in the final analysis, it is only through legal consciousness that constitutional guarantees of rights will become meaningful in people's lives.

Dr. Valery N. Chalidze, a Soviet physicist and Expert-Member of the Moscow Human Rights Committee, is now residing in the United States.

'Falseness Has Made Us Lonely...Lonelier'
By Cynthia Buchanan

If failure is a kind of death, we kill ourselves a thousand times a day when we fall short of our own braggadocio. What is this love of style? Why is the beautiful confused with the good? And even now, on the lip of the Organic Age, why do we continue to praise the contrived? Why is it shameful for a person to be awkward? Why do we disparage him if he is inarticulate? What have we done to the man who, although outside the reach of change, is none the less a man?

How much strife has been introduced into our already fitful hearts by this craving for demeanor cannot be told. Packaging performance, image have made us, as individuals, false. Falseness has made us lonely . . . lonelier.

All the cunning and jockeying of the sexes is only one fume from the anxiety. What have Hemingway and Hefner and Bogart and (even) John Kennedy and Charles Atlas and the sins of their fathers before them done to our males that they continue to labor under their own ghostly machismo?—which must be the loneliest, most fragile state in the world, this worship of form without content. Which is not to say that when the New Woman turns out the light and lies alone upon her night-time bed that the darkness is any the less darkness: it's not that much fun to be right when there's no one there.

Our loneliness anxiety grows out of this gulf between what we are and what we pretend to be, while we tend to define our failure in terms of others' successes. Watered by the media, there is some problem now as to where our values originate. Our native clumsiness—and, moreover, our need of each other and each others' approval—generates a confusion based in a mystique.

Why, indeed, should the ugly be beautiful, the inept, deft or simple people slick? Who knows what monsters Playboy and Cosmopolitan breed in the backwaters by their distortions? The tragedy of Willy Loman was not his obsolescence, his job ending in smoke, his realization that old age was upon him, but rather his yielding to false vision of success.

But our true frangibility as human beings, our true vulgarity can't be subjugated to the symmetry implied in and by technology. As human beings, we are not symmetrical. Our timing is off, our logic lame, our words stand just to one side of the right ones. As Joyce Carol Oates has recognized, "It seems to me that there are so many people who are inarticulate but suffer and doubt and love, nobly, who need to be immortalized or at least explained." In fact, our self-estrangement, our loneliness, often takes the form of great clouds of words. For language, like sex, reminds us we're alive. Instead of demanding that people "say what they mean and mean what they say" (a preposterous request), why do we seldom acknowledge speech as the animal activity it is? Not communication—but a song of ourselves, to ourselves, for the purpose of consoling ourselves. Meanwhile, we strut and charade before our fellows, denying our need, and hoping not to be discovered, as if to be lonely is to be a leperous fool.

Yet still we raise high a dogged American belief in a technical solution for anything.

An ad for computer mating reads: "Cure Loneliness Once and For All!" What kind of a degenerate humanoid could obey that? Why is loneliness treated like psoriasis, a stigma or a birth defect? It is anomalous—and a little embarrassing. Unless it is because loneliness has no place in the *panache* of pop culture. It is beyond culture. And it has never been chic. Loneliness is incorrigible. For it has no answer; it is within life itself.

That we hunger for approval is not news. But that we condemn each other for this hunger is a source of mystery to me. Seeking congruity to assuage our aloneness, like little Genghis Khans, we raid other people—smelling, waiting, tapping for the answers. While we ferret our fellows for an honesty which we ourselves do not display. For it is others-as-mirrors which makes us suspicious. We have been obliged to forsake our true selves, and thus we doubt the veracity of others. But to marry our true selves, we must forgive our false ones, even praise our folly. For nothing is more earnest, more real than falseness, nothing more human. Like narcissism, it is sometimes wistful, child-like. "Look at me!"

We may skirt these people whose slobbering specks our shoetops for their very efforts to draw themselves into history by sage commentaries and diaphanous non sequiturs. But if we would accept the chaos of these unstylish souls, we might learn to accept our own, to operate without judgments of good and bad, and would have less need for self-deception.

Cynthia Buchanan is the author of the novel, "Maiden."

When Smugness Collapsed

By Frances Kaufman

When I lived in Washington—with two babies and my husband, the young sister of a friend came to visit one night. She had just joined a liberation group at the university, and she had a list of complaints about the role of women in contemporary life.

"Why should I marry and have children," she asked, "and why should I marry someone who doesn't want to share the responsibilities of home and family with me? And why should a man's career and identity be more important than mine?"

The answer, I informed her smugly, was not to get so worked up about abstract concepts, and to choose wisely. Not all men, I informed her, make slaves of women; not all women had to have children; and, once women did have children, they had other choices besides full-time baby-sitting and drudgery.

First, motherhood has many satisfactions; second, if you play it wisely, you can always hire someone else to take care of the drudgery part; third, any man worthy of marriage to a woman like her had to understand her needs, and surely, would be more than happy to share the domestic responsibilities; and fourth, she could always choose to do what I was doing and have the best of all possible situations.

After all, I had a well-paying part-time job that allowed me to use my skills, and only took up twenty hours of the week, thereby leaving me with plenty of time for all the creative, pleasant things that life has to offer. Who'd want the obligations of supporting a family or working full time? Not I. I considered myself pretty free: my husband, a self-declared "feminist," was happy to see me working and satisfied, my children were young enough to be sleeping, eating, or otherwise occupied and distracted for the few hours I was away each day, and, because my salary afforded me the luxury of a full-time babysitter/housekeeper, I had plenty of time left to read books, listen to

96

music, romp with the children, participate in the peace movement, even take an acting class or a long walk whenever I felt like it.

By the end of the evening, I had almost converted my young friend.

"Maybe," she thought, "there is hope."

Marguerite, wherever you are, I apologize. My "feminist" husband came home one night and announced that New York beckoned. He had been offered a better paying job with an expanding company that would afford *him* the chance to really grow professionally, and to provide *us* with a "better" way of life.

I objected—we already had a pretty comfortable way of life; all our material needs were satisfied, and we certainly didn't need more possessions; New York was a harder city to raise children in; I couldn't possibly live as close to my work as I did in Washington, where it took only fifteen minutes to travel to work; his entire raise in salary would only cover the higher cost of living in New York; and, besides, in a city crawling with writers and editors, who'd hire me? And who'd be willing to let me name my own hours and conditions of work?

When my objections failed to convince him, I kicked and screamed, held on by my fingernails while he tugged away at my confidence, and then, when all else failed, I flatly refused to leave. He, being a man first (a position far higher, I've discovered, on his list of priorities than that of feminist), and secure in the knowledge that his career and his happiness came first, assured me that he loved me, loved our children, needed all of us, but would somehow learn to manage without us if we chose not to join him in New York.

The battle was won. That kind of pressure I was in no way equipped to withstand. Wasn't I being selfish, trying to force my husband to give up what he wanted because I liked something better? Wasn't I creating grand issues where insignificant ones existed? And, worst, most devastating argument of them all, wasn't I trying to undermine his masculinity?

We moved. And my name went on the ever-growing list of the unemployed.

I have spent the last two years rationalizing all the problems away. I have joined committees that meet during the three hours the children are now in school. I have used up countless hours sewing clothes I don't need and probably will never wear (I'm awful seamstress and nothing I make ever fits anyway); but it fills the time. I read endlessly, can even recite from memory the ingredients on the "King Vitamin" box. I take an occasional day off and haunt the museums, art galleries, movie theaters. I am, as they say, "up on things."

But, let me tell you, I'm lost. And I was probably lost, not at that crucial decision-making time two years ago, but long before I ever agreed to give up my career plans and teach school so that my new husband could finish his graduate work twelve years ago. I am definitely *not* one of the Pepsi generation, or the liberated generation; I belong, most certainly, to the last of the schlepp generation—two years too old for the pill, the Peace Corps, real liberation.

I don't know what the answers are. If I did, I wouldn't find myself wondering, in near-terror, what to do with myself on days when both my children are invited to friends' houses after school on the same day, and being furious that I have allowed myself to be lured into this trap; that I've let my life become so circumscribed that I have nothing to do some days. What I do know is that there will have to be major changes in the way we all live before anything changes.

Change will come only if they transcend the jargon of "concern" for cosmic problems as a substitute for sharing and loving and taking responsibility in their personal affairs. But if change is impossible, if we can't restructure things, then stop lying to us! It's a painful ruse. The women of my generation were not prepared for life. The realities of existence were not part of our training and education. We're not equipped to function in the lives we live.

Frances Kaufman is a writer living now in New York.

The Frances Kaufman Letters

'I cannot sympathize'

To the Editor:

I too am a member of Frances Kaufman's "schlepp generation" ("When Smugness Collapsed," Op-Ed, Feb. 7, 1972). I too was unprepared, both by education and family background, for the "realities of existence," for life as a "liberated woman." But I've learned a lot in twenty years.

If she's a writer, why isn't she freelancing articles or writing stories? Could she go to graduate school? At the very least she could take a volunteer job which would use her skills, and add to her credentials. Until Ms. Kaufman convinces me she's tried all possibilities, I cannot sympathize with her.

MARY LOUISE WILLEY

'A self-pitying complaint'

To the Editor:

Oh, my God! Another one of those whining, self-pitying complaints from a middle-class, educated, talented woman about how society oppresses her! Did it ever occur to her that the man she married might just happen to be a selfish, self-centered, thoughtless human being as well as the product of a system she deplores? Perhaps not! To acknowledge that might be too much of an additional burden to an already-bruised ego.

JOEL POMERANTZ

'Stop shrieking'

To the Editor:

For one thing, she could stop shrieking, get off her pops, and get a job. Any job, if she's really "near terror" during the long afternoons. I cannot believe that in the whole great big city she cannot find the suitable means of enjoying life and feeling self-satisfaction.

EILEEN D. OBSER

'Everyone loses'

To the Editor:

It is not only the women of Frances Kaufman's generation who were unprepared for life. Everyone, men and women, are products of sexist society wherein only half the choices are open to each. The dichotomous conditioning process begins operating soon after birth — half the population is taught to dominate and be self-sufficient, the other half to nurture and submit. Everyone loses in the process and only with great effort do some people achieve a wholeness defined by humanity rather than by culturally defined sex role.

MARILYN SCHAPIRO

'Women's tyranny'

To the Editor:

Equality is equality. Ms. Kaufman was happy in Washington. Apparently Mr. Kaufman was not. Fair? Not by my equality standards. Because her husband sought a better position for himself, and she is having difficulty adjusting to a new situation, she should not snivel. To my mind, Ms. Kaufman is practicing women's tyranny, not liberation.

ALICE D'ANGELO

'Is a wife a slave?'

To the Editor:

Shame on Mrs. Frances Kaufman. She and all the would-be female liberationists overlook or ignore the specific freedom we wives have which is denied to our breadwinner husbands — the freedom of choice. Is a wife a slave because she has to run a household with all its concomitant duties?

DOROTHY H. HUGHES

'She is lost'

To the Editor:

Alas, poor Mrs. Kaufman, she is more lost than she realizes. She states emphatically she is not a member of the Pepsi generation, says she is not a member of the liberated generation and fears she is a member of the schlepp generation. She isn't.

She feels the women of her generation "weren't prepared for life." (Is anyone prepared for life?) Maybe it was being born in the Depression (or raised during it) or growing up during World War II — whatever the reasons — the schlepp generation did not expect life to be rosy and has coped with the realities amazingly well and is still plugging.

ELIZABETH B. MOYNIHAN

'Man and drudgery'

To the Editor:

Frances Kaufman and countless feminists along with her speak of the drudgery involved in being a housewife. Have these ladies thought about the drudgery in the jobs they take to liberate them? Also, but far more important, have they thought about the drudgery their husbands experience on their jobs?

NICKY SCHWARZ

'Lucky Mrs. Kaufman'

To the Editor:

I wonder how many men who aspire to write are in that situation the country over — working for small town papers or local magazines, trapped in the hinterlands by a wife, children, house with mortgage and a job that does afford a living, so that they don't dare give it up without the assurance of another one. Perhaps only persons who are or have been in that situation can realize how lucky Mrs. Kaufman is to have a breadwinner to pay the bills while she attacks the big market.

GLADYS DENNY SHULTZ

'I can sympathize'

To the Editor:

I can sympathize with Mrs. Kaufman but I am happy to say that she does not speak for me or for the many women like me who live happily in schleppdom.

NANCY JOLINE

Formidable Jargon

By Mary Jane Sherfey

Freud was no male chauvinist; and his 1905 female theory was firmly grounded in accepted biology. Not Freud, but the biologists of recent years are at fault—if fault must be found.

Nineteenth-century embryologists established that early mammalian embryos (including man's) were sexually undifferentiated, bisexual, or neutral. Embryos have a large genital tubercle which becomes the penis in males and clitoris in females. No one doubted that the clitoris was a rudimentary penis. Recognizing clitoral stimulation as universal in girls, Freud concluded that girls are born with the capacity of clitoral eroticism and, during childhood, must transfer it to the vagina. Thus, mature women were vaginal and feminine; immature woman, clitoral and masculine.

Biology supported Freud until about 1930 discovering the sex hormones (androgens, male; estrogens, female) with their antagonistic actions ("neutralizing" each other). But the 1940's brought the startling truth: initially all mammalian embryos are females. The penis is an enlarged clitoris.

No conscious efforts were made to conceal this Adam-out-of-Eve finding yet for 25 years it remained the best-kept secret in the history of biology. Even when a logical explanation appeared in 1947 no one noticed that science was rewriting the creation myth.

The explanation involves the evolution of egg-laying to live-bearing animals. Embryos begin with an inactive, bisexual ovotestes. In mammals sex is set by the male chromosome. It induces the ovotestes to become active testes, starting at the seventh week in man. Fetal androgens then veer the innate female anatomy and neutral sexual centers into the male form. With no male chromosome, ovotestes become inactive ovaries. The innate female anatomy continues to unfold by the mother's circulating estrogens. If mammalian reproductive tracts minus ovotestes are removed and kept alive in tissue culture media, they all become female regardless of genetic sex.

Egg-layers' embryos (reptiles, birds, etc.) are innately males with sex determined by the female chromosome. It induces active ovaries and inactive testes. Safe in their shells, males are unexposed to maternal estrogens. Fetal estrogens then veer the male anatomy into the female form. But this ancient arrangement precluded intramaternal existence without shells. Exposed to maternal estrogens males would be feminized and sterile.

In some ancestral species the change happened and prolonged pregnancies became possible. With an innate female anatomy, testes of genetic males secrete sufficient androgens to counterbalance the mother's estrogens.

Longer pregnancies encouraged larger offspring; smaller litters, more complicated brain development, deeper mother-infant ties, and closer family life. They also fostered greater vulnerability of pregnant females, limitations on her other activities, and high survival value for the caring, protective male. Therefore the necessary but not sufficient precondition for mankind's high intelligence and socialization is the prolonged pregnancy which depends upon males being transformed females.

This research was never publicized. For a year I tried to comprehend its formidable jargon. Not until I read this statement: "The neuter sex is female." did it dawn on me that biologists were making no effort to face the implication of their findings. No one wanted the dubious distinction of announcing to the world that the rib belonged to Eve.

I published this data in a Freudian journal in 1966. The biological facts have appeared in a few professional journals since, usually buried in articles on sexual identity. The relevance to the creation myth has hardly been mentioned, let alone elaborated. Not until the feminists picked it up about two years ago from the '66 article, did any segment of the population become aware of the female-first biology, but they spoiled their case by using it in a foolish attempt to discredit all of Freud.

How important are myths? Scientists are often berated for being myth-breakers and they pride themselves on their demythologizing.

Yet judging from the biologists in this bit of biological history, one could conclude that no amount of factual science can pry a man loose from a myth he is not ready to let go. In general, myths are a cornerstone in the edifice of each man's identity.

Dr. Mary Jane Sherfey, author of "The Nature and Evolution of Female Sexuality," is a psychiatrist.

Liberation: A Simultaneous Happening

By Anais Nin

LOS ANGELES—In the forties I wrote despairingly in my diary: "Woman will be the last one on earth to find independence and to find strength in herself." I was judging from the lives of women around me, and from my own. But I was wrong. Several developments accelerated the growth and expansion of woman. One was psychoanalysis, which gave her self-confidence and guidance in the creation of herself as an individual. That was the inner journey that I (and many other women) took. That was the inner journey which women are responding to in the reading of my diaries. They write me: "You affirmed life, affirmed womanhood, affirmed the creative process. You have brought to consciousness in a unique way, the multilevel of woman."

The second development was political; women working in groups and organized efforts to change laws detrimental to the equality of woman, her economic independence, her happiness.

The third was the formation of consciousness-raising groups. Women gathered to discuss their problems openly, to discuss solutions, to strengthen each other's confidence, to establish solidarity.

Each one contributed to the complex problem of liberation which could not be achieved by any one single method. There had to be a synthesis of psychological and political efforts. Newspapers sprang up in every city devoted to the activities of women, their griefs, their frustrations. Magazines were created which focused on the modern woman. Books were written, critical studies of the ideologies of men, of fiction in which woman was denigrated. But more important than attacks upon past ideologies was the formation of new patterns for women. D. H. Lawrence had written that the patterns for women were created by men. Women are now creating their own patterns.

This collective study, examination of past values, revaluations of old patterns, challenge woman's place, woman's character and her potentialities. It accelerated the process of birth in woman, birth of herself as an individual. One woman wrote to me: "We are giving birth to each other."

The "Second Wave" published by a female liberation group of Boston contains thoughtful articles on many subjects never discussed before.

"New Woman," is a magazine as different as possible from "Mademoiselle" and "Glamour" magazines. A profile of Katharine Hepburn focuses on her independence, individuality and courage.

"Black Maria," from Chicago, is filled with well written, lucid articles on subjects vital to women.

Doloris Holmes, art ecologist, is editor of a book to be published soon on eleven women artists. The book is based on interviews made under the auspices of Archives of American Art Grant from New York State Council. She is one of the original women involved in Women Artists in Revolution which publishes her story. Women artists have gathered in Los Angeles under the guidance of Judy Chicago and Mimi Shapiro to practice their art independently of men's teaching.

The magazine-newspaper "Everywoman" in Los Angeles attracts good writers, has its own bookshop for women, and is starting a book of the month club for women writers.

Innumerable courses in women's writing and historical

role have sprung up in colleges. There was a need of historical perspective and balance. Often the role of woman was kept in shadow. A startling example of this is the recent discovery of the letters of Madame Lafayette, whose role was a vital as her husband's in the history of Franco-American relations.

If at first the movement seems to stress separatism, it is a transitional need. Men also for centuries had their clubs, their meetings and conferences closed to women.

As I said in an interview for "New Woman:" "We cannot get rid of the persona (false roles) until we find the fear and self-doubt which makes us create it. Since woman has had more self-doubt and less self-confidence and less time to create her own individuality, she has been more dependent on the persona. Psychology helps us to get rid of the false selves which are built by the family, by tradition, by religion, by the first marriage."

As in all revolutions, the bitter, the defeated, the raucous, the distorted elements are taken up by the press and presented as a true portrait. But too much has happened which will defeat caricature, and too many intelligent women have involved men in this movement which confirms the wise discovery we have made in this century, that liberation can only happen simultaneously to all of us or not at all.

Anaïs Nin is a novelist and diarist.

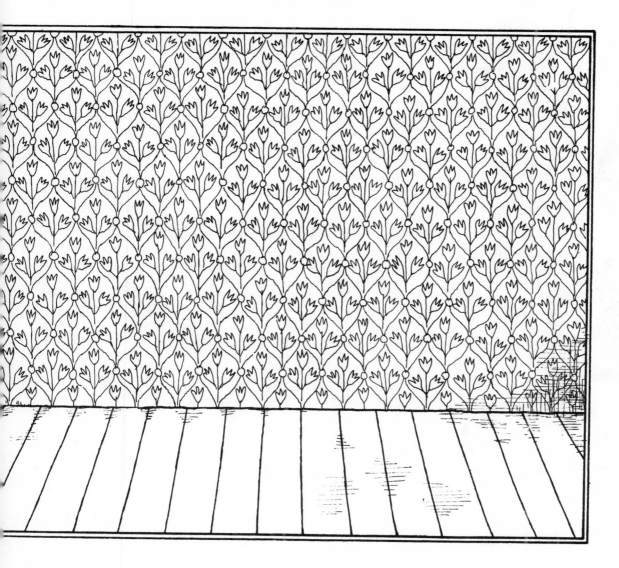

When Felony Had Style

By Jack Finney

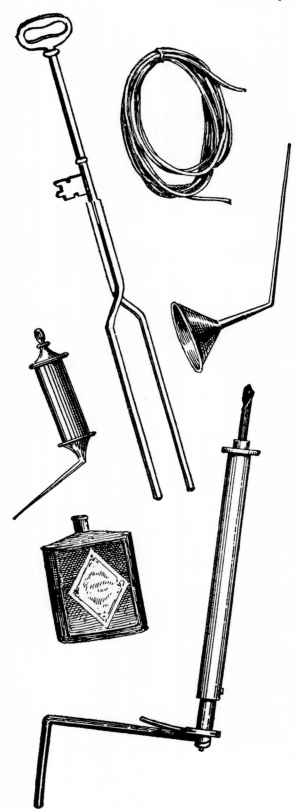

I complain, Mayor Lindsay, not that crime in New York has increased but that its quality has deteriorated. And to that I offer the testimony of Thomas Byrnes, famous nineteenth-century head of the New York cops, one of the first to publish photographs with dossiers—of what must have been some of his favorite crooks and methods. Even routine burglars were craftsmen then, often ingeniously designing their own tools, which Inspector Byrnes shows us (almost proudly, I think). And if one thing didn't work, something else was bound to.

As for the people who committed the crimes that made Byrnes's life so full, there is John Larney, for example, below at the left. He won his alias as a small, sweet-faced boy who disguised himself as a match girl, attended a big outdoor New York shindig, and picked $2,000 worth of pockets. Came the Civil War, and he patriotically enlisted, not once but 93 times, collecting a cash bonus for each. Later, in prison, his eyesight tragically failing, he was given freedom of the jailyard, and climbed the wall, regaining liberty and eyesight simultaneously.

The man beside him, Horace Hovan, would register at a hotel with his wife, then hire a carriage and driver a day or so later. His brother, who looked very like him, and whose voice and mannerisms were identical, would appear, and with a pleasant word for all take Horace's wife for a drive. Meanwhile, Horace was busy distracting a bank clerk, and helping himself to a handful of cash from the till. "Horace Hovan," said Inspector Byrnes, "is without doubt one of the smartest bank sneaks in the world."

James Lee, below at left, is apparently still in the custom-house uniform he wore when rapping at the doors of New York houses. A "package from Europe" had arrived, he'd say, and $9.98 was due; never more or less. The lady of the house got a receipt good for the package at the custom house. While waiting Lee would sometimes sit down at piano or organ, says Byrnes, and play, "Nearer, my God, to Thee."

The man beside Lee is "Lord Courteney, the bogus British nobleman, well known in New York . . . ." He was "34 . . . born in England . . . slim . . . six-foot-two . . . dark hair, heavy eyes. . . . " And in the Royal Navy uniform he is wearing here, he not only conned New Yorkers and others out of wads of cash, but "delighted and infatuated the young ladies" who cut his uniform buttons off for souvenirs.

Dave Cummings, below at left, became fascinated with the sight of a safe standing in a pool of light each night behind the glass door of a well-known jewelry store. Dave made a fine-looking duplicate, switched it with the real safe, which he trundled to the back room, and relieved of $100,000 in diamonds and jewelry, not a nickel ever recovered.

The modern-looking fellow, above at right, was a "terrible talker," says Byrnes. He must have been, because he charmed no less than Oscar Wilde, who was visiting the States. For a week they were chums, lunching and dining together at the famous Brunswick Hotel. The friendship broke up when Hungry Joe conned Oscar out of $5,000, which Oscar paid with a rubber check.

Okay, Women's Lib, *okay*! Sophie Lyons "blackmailed scores of businessmen" by somehow persuading them to remove their clothes, playfully hiding them, then selling them back for prices like $10,000. When one stubborn man got back his clothes, and left without paying, good old Sophie "made a daily practice of sitting on a horse-block in front of the residence of one of her Grand Rapids, Mich., victims, who was a very prominent man. He got rid of Mrs. Lyons by turning the hose on her, and pounding an unfortunate theatrical agent who espoused her quarrel."

"Little Louise," ladylike in manner and appearance," went to Brazil as companion to a rich Spanish woman, stole the lady's diamonds, was caught, given forty lashes and had the bottom of her right ear cut off. She got a new hair-do, covering her ears, and became "one of the smartest female pickpockets in this country."

Byrnes even had an ex-Governor of South Carolina to watch out for, and a graduate of Corpus Christi College, Oxford, Edward Fairbrother. He had an M.D. degree, spoke five languages, came to New York to practice medicine and, he said, "I had no disposition for crime. But time's whirligig turned me up a criminal; and I fought hard against it, too." Losing the fight, however, he—what? Snatched an old lady's pocketbook? Robbed a pay phone? No, sir, John V. L., not a gent like this; he stole $6,000 in diamonds from the residence of the Mayor of New York.

Jack Finney, author of "Time and Again," is in love with Old New York.

The burglars' tools are from Helen Campbell's "Darkness and Daylight or Lights and Shadows of New York Life," published in 1897. The portraits are from "Professional Criminals of America," by Thomas Byrnes, published in 1886.

Sophie Lyons
Alias Levy
Pickpocket and Blackmailer

Louisa Jourdan
Alias Little Louise
Pickpocket and Shop Lifter

John Larney
Alias Mollie Matches
Bank Sneak and Burglar

Horace Hoven
Alias Little Horace
Bank Sneak

Franklin J. Moses
Alias Ex. Gov. Moses
Swindler

Edward Fairbrother
Alias Doctor West
Hotel Thief

Dave Cummings
Alias Hogan
Hotel Thief

Joseph Lewis
Alias Hungry Joe
Banco

James Lee
Bogus Custom House
Collector

Hugh L. Courtenay
Alias Lord Courtenay
Swindler

103

In Memory of Seymour Schneider

By Peter Schneider

I wish to report that my brother has been murdered.

On the afternoon of Sept. 2, 1971—a few days short of his 49th birthday—my brother, Seymour Schneider, who in his lifetime had never raised a hand in violence against another, was shot in the head twice and robbed in his auto sales office on Bruckner Boulevard in the Bronx.

The lives of many will be diminished because of his death—his wife to whom he was devoted, his children to whom he was dedicated, his brothers and sisters to whom he was loyal, his relatives and friends to whom he brought a lightness of spirit, a measure of joy and a manner that was carefree, though his life was not.

But, from all the rest of the world he slipped silently away, in spite of the sound of the bullets that shattered his skull, for his murder was not deemed worthy of note in our press.

A man is killed in broad daylight in his street-floor office on a main roadway in the city, and compounding the horror of the homicide is that, outside of his family and friends, the event is unnoticed.

Murder has become commonplace. It has joined the crimes of mugging and rape in occurring with such frequency that newspapers seldom report them. When I went to the medical examiner's office to identify his body, I was given a number to await my turn, as we are given numbers in a busy retail shop.

Fifteen hundred such murders a year, many thousands of vicious muggings on our streets and in the lobbies of our houses, and with it all we go through the routine of daily existence. How long can people survive in this jungle of violence, terror and fear? How many more casualties must we suffer before we recognize that we cannot live this way?

Two of my three sisters have been mugged and assaulted, and now one of my brothers has been murdered and robbed. Who is next in this game of New York roulette? And where shall we seek a solution, when with a clearance rate of only 10 per cent of our felonies—that is, one out of ten serious crimes results in an arrest—our courts are overwhelmed and overburdened; our jails are overcrowded and ineffectual, with reformatories that do not reform, correction institutes that do not correct, prisons that are schools for advanced criminal techniques and that graduate tough, embittered enemies of society who are paroled because there is no room to keep them.

Terror and fear stride our streets. Amid this chaos we are asked to admire a mayor for his courage in walking through the streets of our ghettos—accompanied by policemen, press and politicians—when all we ask for ourselves is to feel safe to walk to the nearest subway station in our neighborhood.

Our mayor and his police commissioner divert us with their quixotic—and sometimes cruel—political antics with police department personnel.

They have inveighed against police corruption and they have forced out of the police department a number of high-ranking officers, and in the public's mind these acts were related. I knew some of these officers to be men of integrity and probity and I see politics in these events.

Our No. 1 police problem in the city is crime in the streets. Our homes have become fortresses, our defenses pick-proof locks, barred windows and burglar-alarm systems. Our streets are paths through a mined no-man's land.

The failure of the mayor and police commissioner to address themselves to the problems of murder and mugging is another type of corruption. They are willing to create the illusion of acting on the problem foremost in the public's mind, when what they are actually doing is diverting our attention from that problem—and in the process destroying the careers of some good men.

We would be more impressed with the police commissioner's announced performance-rating system for his commanding officers if he applied it where it would have immediate significance: to crimes of violence.

There is a word that everyone has used to describe my brother's death—senseless. It was senseless in that the murderer could have achieved his robbery without having committed this savage murder. But from the view that the act fits a pattern of conduct that we have begun to see repeatedly, a pattern of insane fury, of maddened violence by subhuman creatures, it had the sense of patterned conduct.

For the grotesque, the monstrous, the aberrant, the perverted, have become the common and the commonplace, the usual and—God help us!—the expected.

My brother was one more victim. Who among us is next?

Peter Schneider is a New York lawyer.

Other Days and Other Crimes

By Irene Fischl

Whenever I read of a fresh outburst of racial violence in one of the city's schools, my mind goes back to an incident that took place in the nineteen-forties during my eighth year of school in a working class neighborhood in Brooklyn.

There were 28 children in my class and all but four were Jewish. Our teachers were Jewish or Irish Catholic. We had been together, students and teachers, for two years, a deliberate plan to bring continuity to our relationships with our teachers and with each other. We were a tightly knit group forming deep—and we thought lifelong—friendship. We had teachers who knew us well and gave a great deal of themselves. In this womb-like environment, days were peaceful. I can still remember the one act of delinquency that was committed in all of those two years. A boy—his name comes back as though it were yesterday—threw a blackboard eraser at his friend in a spirit of mischief. He was made to stand in front of the room, his face blanching and his eyes downcast, where he was held up before us by the outraged teacher as a boy who, by his thoughtless deed, "could have taken someone's eye out." That was the worst act of disruption I ever witnessed.

We had a music teacher named Marguerite O'Shea. Miss O'Shea had eyes the color of aquamarine gems, a rose-flushed complexion, and hair that was prematurely gray. On special occasions she wore a velvet dress—it was my favorite—in a color that matched her eyes, with a large white hand-crocheted collar which fell almost to her waist. And under that collar, we speculated after hours, rested the most beautiful bosom in the world. Miss O'Shea loved us, and we loved her. We loved her for her Irish good looks, her pleasant ways, and for the fun we had in her classroom, singing and listening to her play the piano.

Just about this time, Miss O'Shea began to teach us a series of hymns, and as the semester progressed, the hymns became more and more Catholic. At the same time, most of the boys in the class were preparing for their Bar Mitzvahs, the Jewish coming-of-age ceremony, and they were undergoing a sort of consciousness-raising. Before this, none of us had thought too much about Jewish identity. Now the boys were troubled. In public school they were singing hymns to Jesus. In religious school they were being reminded of their Jewish heritage.

In the posse that walked home together after school each day, we discussed our dilemma and hit on a plan of action. We selected the sweetest, most well-groomed, gentlemanly boy in our number as our spokesman. The next day in music class, while Miss O'Shea sounded the notes of a hymn about the evils of blasphemy on the piano, and while our hearts thumped, Harold raised his hand: "Miss O'Shea," he said somberly, "we boys are being Bar Mitz-

vahed this year and we don't feel right about singing hymns to Jesus."

A flicker of shocked surprise, followed by one of pain, crossed her beautiful face—not pain because we didn't want to sing about Jesus, but because it had suddenly occurred to her that perhaps she had wronged us. In that instant, it was apparent, even to a roomful of thirteen-year-olds, that she had taught us the hymns because she thought they were beautiful and that this possible conflict had never entered her mind. "I understand," she said softly, managing to look at each of us directly. And we knew she did understand.

From then on the hymns grew more ecumenical, and we resumed learning and singing with gusto.

It was against this backdrop that I read with some sadness of a confrontation, nineteen-seventies-style, between Jewish students led by Rabbi Meir Kahane, and black students on the campus of my alma mater, Brooklyn College.

It, too, was a squabble about who calls the tune. On a jukebox in the student canteen, Jewish students were playing an Israeli song, "Next Year in Jerusalem," the one that forms the musical background of a recent El Al television commercial. From varying reports pieced together, it seems they played it six or seven times in succession and this irritated the black students. There were words, some say insults, then the black students were supposed to have broken into the jukebox and destroyed the record.

A few days later, some 100 Jewish students and Jewish Defense Leaguers led by Meir Kahane returned to the canteen. Rabbi Kahane is reported to have said: "Let's give them a live performance." The group sang "Next Year in Jerusalem" and other Israeli songs. Then they started moving some tables out of the way to make room for a dance.

One white girl thinks the sparks began to fly when the Jewish students encroached on black turf. "They crossed the invisible line," she said. Blacks claim they were pushed out. Push turned to shove. Fists flew. Tables, chairs and belt buckles became weapons.

I couldn't help but wonder what would have happened if Miss O'Shea and Harold had been around instead of Meir Kahane and the goons on both sides. The black students might have selected the sweetest, most gentlemanly boy in their number, who might approach a Jewish kid and say: "Hey man, do you have to play that same song over and over again?" To which the Jewish kid might have replied: "I understand."

Irene Fischl is author of "Love Is When You Meet a Man Who Doesn't Live With His Mother."

Straight to the Vein

By Sandy Smith

At the age of 17 I had a habit. I was addicted to heroin. I began using heroin shortly after my 17th birthday at the insistence of a friend who had long been going that route himself.

For me there was no going from reefers to sniffing and then to mainlining. I went straight to the vein in my left arm, just above the elbow. I first placed the needle (in what is known as the *pit*) and introduced heroin into my bloodstream and system.

After twenty years of off-again-on-again use of heroin, I found and still find that it is nearly as easy to obtain as marijuana. Outlawed as it may be, it is so very readily available that any child can obtain it within actual feet of his or her school.

Growing up as a young black man who was hooked on drugs, I knew that it was wrong, but I also knew that blacks are, by the very nature of their forced existence, in no way able to handle or control, that they are jail prone. Blacks are largely unable to get decent jobs and are forced to make their living in the streets.

I got to like what it was that I was doing and soon found that I could not stop doing it. I was "hooked" and could not think of doing anything else but going the way of the "spike." The more I believed that I could stop or quit when and if I wanted to, the more firmly I became entrenched in the cycle of drug abuse.

I had taken the first shot of dope when I was 17 and it had somehow lasted for some twenty years, not counting the years I spent in jail. Although I shot no dope when I was in jail, I waited for the day when I would get out so I could get to a syringe full of the "stuff."

I have been sorry ever since that first shot although even now if I let down my guard for one minute I would be right back at it. Like an alcoholic, it is not the tenth or the twelfth shot that hooks you, but the very first. And there is no let-up in the wanting of the beautiful euphoric state that one can experience from the shot.

I finally realized that there was a plot and plan to contain drug use within black ghettos across the country. It was devised by the very people who are supposedly dedicated to the curtailing of trafficking and abolition of all illicit drug markets! This plot to contain drugs in the black ghettos of the country is an attempt to keep me as a creative person in a total state of flux and to continue to see me (as all other black men) run the circular gamut of the in-again-out-again prison route. I stand witness to this as I have been a guest at the Atlanta Federal Penitentiary, New Jersey's State Prison, Annandale Reformatory, Hudson County Jail, Riker's Island and Sing Sing.

All this has resulted in my finally taking immediate steps to reconstruct my life rather than wait for the system to do it for me. While in each of those concentration camps I found not a whit of rehabilitory assistance offered to me or any of the other men detained in them. In order to attain any form of rehabilitation in today's penal colonies, one must take it upon himself to construct his own program. That is the only way to achieve sanity, sobriety and usefulness to himself and to his loved ones. The prison system does not aid in this at all. The prison system only concerns itself with the detaining of the prisoner until such time as its (the system's) laws say that the prisoner can be released to return to the same society that has seen him or her, by default of race, go into the concentration camp in the first instance.

Sandy Smith was a writer, ex-convict and drug addict who died in June, 1972 of a drug overdose.

Saturday's Mother

By Anne Levine

"Ma?"

My heart sinks as I hear my daughter's voice on the phone. One short word and I know that Linda is on pills again. Her voice, usually soft and sweet, sounds hoarse and dully belligerent, which means that she is on "downs." Linda boasts to her friends that her mother knows if she even takes aspirin.

Even though I am positive that she has taken a large dose, I try to speak calmly. I don't want to play games again, she denying that she is high and me insisting that she is. I know Linda too well.

"Linda, where are you?"

"I'm at a friend's house."

"Come home. You don't sound well at all."

"I have no transportation and I have no money."

"Tell me where you are and I will pick you up."

"No!"

"Then why did you call me? Just to worry me?" Now I completely lose control of my emotions. I scream at her: "You promised you wouldn't take pills any more!"

No reply, just a click at the other end of the phone.

A cold, drizzly Saturday morning in April and the weather matches my uneasiness. Where is she? Would she get home safely? I am not angry any more. My heart goes out to my child. In my mind I see her; her face pale, her hair disheveled, her bright eyes now dull and heavy. The pills alter her personality and change her appearance.

An hour later the phone rings. I am afraid to answer it. I sense trouble. It is only my mother. We talk about the rotten weather and she says I sound as if I am upset. I tell her I am probably getting a cold. She asks how Linda is and I say she is fine. So many lies to cover up my daughter's problems. My mother is old. I don't want to worry her. Most important, I don't want pity.

Again the phone rings; my premonition becomes a reality. It is the local hospital.

"Is this Linda's mother?"

"Yes, what happened to my daughter?"

"Linda stumbled in the street and came to the Emergency Room to have her knee treated. She passed out while the doctor was taking care of her. We think she is on drugs. Would you please come to the hospital?"

Strange, I feel no emotion. I don't panic. I don't cry. It is as if my heart closes shop for a while, to let my brain take over so that I can function rationally.

My husband is away on business. I am too ashamed to ask anyone to come with me to the hospital. Every time Linda takes pills I feel as guilty as if I handed them to her. Philosophers may blame society for today's drug scene but mothers blame themselves.

Now the drizzle becomes a morbid downpour, a suitable background for my fear.

I go to the hospital. The nurse leads me to a small treatment room. Linda lies sleeping quietly on a table. The room seems vaguely familiar.

The young doctor is sympathetic. He says that when Linda wakes up she will be sent to the County Hospital for psychiatric examination. It is the law.

This is not the first time Linda has taken an overdose but she always manages to come home. I know she will sleep deeply for about twelve hours as the pills slowly drain out of her body.

I sit down by Linda's side and watch her sleep. I am grateful to feel numb. I want to remain numb; to feel is too painful.

The room is still, only the sound of Linda's gentle breathing. I look around, convinced now that I have been in this room before. And then I remember; many years ago this part of the hospital had been the maternity section. I had labored to give birth to Linda in this very room seventeen years ago. I remember how happy I was then.

Linda woke up in the evening. She looked around and then she saw me quietly sitting there, and in a hoarse voice said, "I feel O.K. I want to go home."

"Linda, you can't go home just now. They say you have to go to the county hospital for a psychiatric examination. Perhaps it is for the best. The ambulance will be here soon."

My daughter turned her head away. We were not playing games any more.

Ambulance attendants are businesslike. No one spoke a word as we rode the short distance to the County Hospital.

As the ambulance drove up the driveway and the attendant prepared to open the double doors Linda took my hand. "Mommy, I am so scared. Please stay with me. I'm so sorry."

And then we both cried, at last.

Anne Levine is a pseudonym for a woman living and writing in New York.

'A Loneliness I Never Expected'

By Ralph Cokain

Arranging for her funeral while she lay in a coma with death imminent was an activity I find hard to believe I went through. It was the last thing in the world I had ever wanted to do, but it had to be done, although I was still too dazed to fully comprehend the impact of losing the person in the world I loved most dearly.

We had shared so many years together, we had shared so many wonderful and exciting experiences, we were so much in love and such inseparable companions, the very idea that one of us would die and leave the other alone and bereaved seemed so remotely distant that we refused to entertain it and spoil our fun.

We talked a great deal—about ourselves, our relatives, our friends, our jobs, human behavior, politics, current events—nearly everything. I remember one occasion when we were discussing ourselves and our happiness together when the thought suddenly occurred to both of us (we frequently had the same thought at the same time)—one would die and leave the other alone.

When conversation is cheered by the wonderment of being so happy together, it is not easy and seems unduly morbid to introduce the topic of inevitable death. But it was on our minds and I hesitantly broached the subject by announcing the funeral home I wanted to conduct my services. Until that moment it had always been my intention, since I found the subject so abhorrent, to indicate my choice on a slip of paper which she would find after I was gone. But now, with a somewhat shaky voice, I had expressed my preference. She was not surprised; she knew, because it was also her own choice. Now that we understood each other, and since surely there were so many years ahead of us, it was a relief to continue our talk on lighter terms.

As far as I was concerned, the possibility was none other but that I would precede her, so I never gave the least consideration to the idea that she might die first.

After all, wasn't she in excellent health and eleven years my junior? And didn't wives nearly always outlive husbands? I used to try to imagine her looking at my dead countenance, and I shuddered at her sadness and bereavement. But she would have to go through it, there was no way out. Because it appeared so improbable, I felt it unduly morbid to dwell on her earlier demise. Why should I torture myself about something I was reasonably certain would not happen?

Now it is some four or five years later. Come the first day of summer (what irony!) she will have been dead two years.

I miss her terribly and I have agonized—nearly to the point of self-destruction.

I am living a loneliness I never expected. I feel so vulnerable, so inferior, so unsure of myself.

I find no purpose in living, though I have been told that purpose will eventually manifest itself. There are no fond expectations, no stimulating goals, no promising future.

Everything seems different—even the newspaper she loved so much and the news magazine that could disturb her routine if it arrived a day late. We frequented so many places I am constantly reminded of her; the music we shared I cannot bear to hear now. What anguish to come home night after night to an apartment devoid of her warmth and radiance.

Should I take consolation that she was spared the ordeal of losing a loved one? That is quite difficult, for I am beset by doubts and contradictions which leave me with the conclusion that she was too wonderful to die so soon, that she should have lived to the point of surviving as my widow. Perhaps that is selfish reasoning, but in the wake of my deep loss it seems at least conventional.

Ralph Cokain lives and writes in New York.

One Small Life

By Joseph Farkas

MAPLEWOOD, N. J.—After a period of sweltering weather, a bright cool August day dawned over Concord, Mass., in 1853, and Henry Thoreau, who had planned to sit and write in the house all day, decided that it was wiser to spend such a day outdoors. He went for a sail on the Sudbury River with his friend, William Ellery Channing. He later memorialized this glorious day in his journal.

After the recent extended hot spell, Aug. 10 similarly arrived in New Jersey as the first bright day of fall. When I left my desk for a brief outdoor walk I noticed a woodchuck scuttling across the broad lawn in front of my building. When he stopped, with his back toward me, I decided on impulse to see how close I could get to him before he became aware of me and scurried away. I walked quickly toward him until I was about six feet away and stopped. I was surprised that he hadn't detected me, but I soon saw why. He lay there with his head stretched out on the lawn and his eyes closed. He had obviously settled down for a snooze on the sun-warmed grass.

I stood there for about a minute before he suddenly raised his head and looked around at me. After contemplating me over his shoulder awhile, he turned around to face me. Then he sat up on his haunches, as though to get a better view of me.

After we had faced each other for a while, I swayed to left and right to see what effect such movement would have on him. He dropped to all fours, lowered his head, and hissed. His defensive posture indicated a readiness to fight rather than run. I moved back a few paces and then circled in back of him. He turned his head to keep me in view but did not move his body.

As I went back to the sidewalk from which I had started my confrontation I saw a small open truck in the cab of which were three workmen who had been watching the woodchuck and me. When I got alongside the truck one of them offered to give me a club to attack the woodchuck.

When I asked why I should do that, he said woodchucks were becoming too numerous and causing too much damage. They dug up lawns and ate shrubbery.

I said it would nevertheless be nice to leave the woodchuck alone, and walked away. But then I look back and saw the man who had offered me the club walking toward the woodchuck with a four-foot metal pipe in his hand. Sensing what was coming, my first impulse was to turn my back on the scene and continue walking. But I couldn't. I watched the man get to about ten or twelve feet from the victim and stop. He waved the pipe but the woodchuck didn't move. Then the man inexplicably turned around, walked back, and got into the truck, which drove away.

I walked on, but before returning to my office I decided to have another look at my friend the woodchuck. He was still on the lawn. While I was about 200 feet away from him I saw a figure approaching him. It was the man from the truck, this time carrying a long-handled pitchfork. The truck was at the curb.

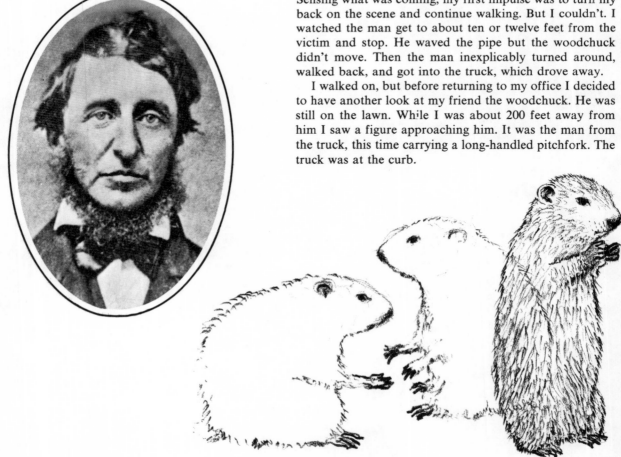

The man walked slowly toward the woodchuck. When he was about ten feet away, the woodchuck started running. The man pursued him. The woodchuck reached a small pine whose branches grew down to the ground and he ducked into it.

The man stalked around the pine, his pitchfork at the ready. Several times he lunged forward but apparently missed his prey. But then he was suddenly pushing hard on the pitchfork, his body bent forward.

After holding this position for perhaps half a minute, he let up. But the job was not yet done. He ran around to the other side of the tree and began jabbing again. The once more he leaned hard on the pitchfork and held his position. When he straightened up I caught a glimpse of a bloody mass writhing at the end of the pine.

The man called to the truck for a shovel. The man from the truck came, not with a shovel but holding a metal pipe. He whacked the woodchuck several times, delivering the *coup de grace*. Then the man with the pitchfork impaled the woodchuck on its tines, held it aloft as he walked back to the truck, and threw it into the back of the truck. The truck drove slowly off.

After dinner I went out to my tree-encircled back yard to savor what was left of this sparkling day. I sat there watching the sunlight playing through the top of the big maple. The sky was cloudless. A helicopter chugged through in one direction and a highflying airliner passed in another.

After sitting awhile, I reread a section of Thoreau's journal describing his encounter with a woodchuck in the spring of 1852. Although I hadn't realized it at the moment I began the episode with my woodchuck, it was residual memory of Thoreau's woodchuck account that had obviously triggered my own adventure.

Thoreau describes how he came across the woodchuck in the middle of a field, pursued it, and then sat down three feet from it when it stopped. It trembled and gritted its teeth. He touched its snout with a twig and it bit the stick. They sat looking at each other for half an hour. Thoreau talked to it in what he called forest baby talk and soothed it enough to enable him to turn it over on its back and even put his hand on it briefly. He thought that if he had had the right food to offer it he could have tamed it completely. Thoreau said that he respected the woodchuck as one of the natives and thought he might learn some wisdom from him.

I also read the journal entry on the beautiful August day of 1853, a day affecting the spirits of men and worthy of a hymn. Thoreau regretted that so few enjoyed such a day. "What do the laborer ox and the laborer man care for the beautiful days? Will the haymaker when he comes home tonight know that this has been such a beautiful day?" Did the woodchuck executioners know when they got home that afternoon that it had been such a beautiful day?

Joseph Farkas is chief historian for the U.S. Army Munitions Command.

And What Would Henry Thoreau Have Thought?

To the Editor:

It struck me while reading Joseph Farkas' "One Small Life" [Op-Ed, Aug. 29] that Thoreau would never have stood around and allowed another man to kill a woodchuck 200 feet away from him.

LINDA CLARKE   New York City

To the Editor:

The account of the killing of the woodchuck and the earlier account of the poodle standing guard over his collie friend killed on the highway [Op-Ed, July 11] are sad commentaries on man's destructiveness. But implicit in both stories is an increasingly frequent, linked observation: the passivity in the face of violence of men of better instincts. Could not Mr. Farkas have done more than just watch the pitchforking of the woodchuck?

JO COUDERT   New York City

To the Editor:

It is quite apparent Mr. Farkas was not brought up on a farm else he would know that the woodchuck is a rodent capable of much damage to crops.

In my vegetable garden a woodchuck has just destroyed seven out of twelve large cabbage plants and has ruined two rows of Swiss Chard.

I am glad to report the villain has been trapped and his remains put to rest without benefit of clergy.

V. R. BLAIR   White Plains, N. Y.

To the Editor:

I would certainly distinguish between woodchucks and human beings, yet I wonder why Mr. Farkas when in no real danger himself would not act to save the woodchuck. I doubt we could count on him when there might be real danger to his own life to resist a wrong to another human being. The point is not whether woodchucks are good or bad animals, nor that those men chose to kill the animal. The point is that Mr. Farkas chose not to act but to watch, record what he saw, and no doubt receive a fat fee from The New York Times for his trouble.

The Mylai massacre mentality is not confined to a distant tiny wartorn land; it lives among us. Does he chief historian of the U.S. Army Munitions Command record the despicable results of our munitions in Vietnam with equal lack of involvement?

And he dare speak the name Thoreau in the same breath.

RICHARD STEINBERGER Princeton, N. J.

To the Editor:

I sat for a long time mulling over this story of brutality to a small creature and wondering what prompted Mr. Farkas to write it.

Was it, perhaps, an attempt to expiate his sin of omission in not intervening in the woodchuck's behalf, or was he merely recording an event while accepting the right of men to destroy creatures whose habits they do not understand or whose existence inconveniences them slightly?

I noticed that Mr. Farkas is connected with the U.S. Army, which turned my thoughts to Vietnam. I think about Vietnam quite a lot during this period of intensive bombing, and I wondered if he might have intended to produce a parable of our involvement there, in order to make more real the cruelty of a few men destroying living beings while our nation stands by and quietly observes.

If that was his intent I wish him success and a wide audience.

MARY SPECHT Huntingdon Valley, Pa.

To the Editor:

At the end of the article, Mr. Farkas wonders if the woodchuck's murderers truly appreciated the beauty of the day. I would wonder if Farkas ever questioned his moral responsibility in this matter. Surely Thoreau, whom the author apparently admires, would have acted differently. Assuming that he wanted to avoid physical confrontation, could not Farkas have been more forceful in his verbal exchange with the workmen? At the very least, he could have chased the animal while the men were choosing their respective weapons.

One cannot help feeling that the author had decided early on to abandon the woodchuck to its fate and to record this event for posterity. To what end?

JUDITH ZINN Hempstead, N. Y.

To the Editor:

What man would not at least have frightened the animal away with a sound—a stone—something that would have given the animal a chance against the executioner?

MARY F. PEO Short Hills, N. J.

Woodchucks in Death and Life

I plead guilty to having stood idly by while a woodchuck was being pitchforked to death. I plead guilty to having done nothing to prevent the killing of over a million people in Vietnam. I plead guilty to countless sins of omission in failing to do anything to correct the injustices, the ugliness, the horrors of the life around us. I respect all those who have actively taken arms against a sea of troubles and attempted, by opposing, to end them. But to the millions who—like me—have out of inertia, cowardice, selfishness, or ignorance given silent assent (or even active support) to the perpetration of evil, I say: Let him who is without sin cast the first stone.

JOSEPH FARKAS Maplewood, N. J., 1972

As I came home through the woods with my string of fish, trailing my pole, it being now quite dark, I caught a glimpse of a woodchuck stealing across my path, and felt a strange thrill of savage delight, and was strongly tempted to seize and devour him raw; not that I was hungry then, except for that wildness which he represented. Once or twice, however, while I lived at the pond, I found myself ranging the woods, like a half-starved hound, with a strange abandonment, seeking some kind of venison which I might devour, and no morsel could have been too savage for me. The wildest scenes had become unaccountably familiar. I found in myself, and still find, an instinct toward a higher, or, as it is named, spiritual life, as do most men, and another toward a primitive rank and savage one, and I reverence them both.

HENRY DAVID THOREAU Walden, Concord, Mass., 1854

The Fifth Horseman Is Riding

By Larry Van Goethem

JANESVILLE, Wis.—When I was a boy growing up in northern Wisconsin it seemed there would be no end to flowing rivers and clear lakes amid the forest.

The Wisconsin landscape, scoured and shaped by the last glacier only 10,000 years ago and then created in greens, browns and blues by the sun, rain, wind and seed, was something special in our lives.

No single Walden Pond here, but hundreds, thousands of lakes speckle the landscape. And the rivers roll and run and roar, at times blue and at times mahogany as root beer, even the foam in rapids root-beer-tinted by the iron deposits in the earth.

Now it is becoming apparent that a crime, a planetary blunder of the first magnitude, is taking place in Wisconsin.

A disaster is happening before our eyes so slowly, so insidiously the impact is somehow lost. The "Land o'Lakes" is falling slow victim to the huckster, the real estate man, the developer, the politician, the industrialist, the tourist and the fisherman, and even the Pentagon.

Wisconsin, so clean and clear and lovely, is being blighted.

Most people recognize or sense what is happening because it happens around them every day, in the cities and prairie vistas of the south and in the lakes midstate.

Hucksters have turned the Wisconsin Dells into a billboard outpost of commercialism; the city of Milwaukee dumps millions of gallons of raw wastes into Lake Michigan every day, a slow stain of pollution creeps further outward toward Lake Michigan from Green Bay fed by the Fox River Valley cities and the largest concentration of paper mills in the world.

The Wisconsin River runs red and brown with pulp paper mill wastes; it is restricted for fishing for a long stretch.

The Horizon National Wildlife Refuge is polluted by the Rock River.

The paper mills resist efforts by the Wisconsin Department of Natural Resources to improve their effluent. So do many other industries.

But the cosmic crime is taking place in the northern lake country. It is a crime because we should know better.

Once secluded northern lakes have become lined with summer homes and cottages. Resorts have sprung up. Unaccountably high levels of mercury have been measured in fish taken from remote lakes and trout streams.

Billboards, neon lights and signposts have turned parts of the lake country into rural slum.

The United States Navy wants to construct a huge communications grid in the lake country to communicate with nuclear submarines in time of war—a doomsday button as one writer described it.

Cottage owners whose septic tanks pollute the waterways fight official attempts to improve their waste-disposal methods. Big power boats ruin vegetation, marine life and spawning beds.

You fish a secluded lake where loons call and an occasional tern breaks water and find that a tiny island in the lake's center is littered with beer and pop cans and bottles.

The facts are here. They are published, catalogued and filed but too often ignored.

It does no good to tell a developer the swamp he is filling for cabins is a vital part of the lake or river adjacent to it. Nor does it help to ask a farmer to fence cattle off from a waterway or provide green space between his crops and rivers or creeks.

A sense of despair pervades because this delicate landscape was a long time in creation—about 10,000 years and we are destroying it so rapidly.

The great rivers of northern Wisconsin fall off an 1,800-foot tableland into Lake Superior and Michigan and the Mississippi River. There are rivers like the Peshtigo, the Menominee, the Popple, Brule, Pine, Flambeau and the Chippewa. We once drank water from them, now we hesitate.

Oh, the Land o'Lakes is still lovely, incomparably so. And the lakes—Thoreau should see them. They plumb deep as a man's mind, shallow as his emotions.

What is difficult is to admit that certain development probably should be discouraged, regulated or outright banned in some primitive areas in order to preserve them.

Should you want to see the lakes, hurry, because the fifth horseman is riding and nobody can rein him in.

Larry Van Goethem is a Wisconsin newspaperman.

The Rebirth of a Future

By Charles A. Reich

Day-to-day events leave us with a feeling of chaos; it seems as if we must be mere powerless spectators at the decline and fall of our country. But these same events are capable of being understood as part of a larger process of social change—a process that is fearsome and yet fundamentally hopeful. And we may be participants—we may regain the power to make our own future—if only we understand what is taking place.

In Spain, the American President rides in an open car with a military dictator who by using lawless force has repressed all meaningful social progress. In Vietnam, halfway around the world, young Americans are compelled to fight in support of another corrupt dictatorship. These are not separate events, they are symptoms of a larger pattern. Women's liberation, black militancy, the campaign against the S.S.T., Gay Liberation, the long hair of youth are not separate events either; they too are related. The many wars, the many revolutions, are one.

The agonies of the great industrial nations, and especially our own, are no mystery. They have been fully predicted and explained by many social thinkers. There is much room for argument among schools of thought, but the main outline is clear. Neither machines nor material progress is inherently bad. But we have achieved our progress by a system which short-sightedly wastes man and nature by failing to protect them in the haste for gain. A rising crime rate, extremes of inequality, neglect of social needs, personal alienation and loss of meaning, disorder and war are all manifestations of the underlying process of corrosive exploitation.

This process has now reached a point where remedial action is desperately urgent. Knowing this, why are we unable to guide our progress along more rational lines? Why is our system so rigid that it ignores even the mild remedies proposed by its own Presidential Commissions? This brings us to a second element of our crisis, an element which also can be explained. American society has been amalgamated into a single monolith of power—the corporate state—which includes both the private and public structures. This monolith is not responsible to democratic or even executive control. The Corporate State is mindless and irrational. It rolls along with a momentum of its own, producing a society that is ever more at war with its own inhabitants. Again, there is plenty of room for different theories of the state, but the major pattern of unthinking and uncontrolled power must by now be accepted.

If our nation's immobility can be explained and understood, we must ask once more: why are we unable to refashion our system? All social systems are merely the creations of men; men make them and men can change them. But the power to act is limited by our consciousness. Today most Americans are not conscious of the realities of their society.

One segment of the American people remains at a level of consciousness that was formed when we were a land of small villages and individual opportunity; Consciousness I is unable to accept the reality of an interdependent society that requires collective responsibility. A second segment of the American people understands the realities of organization life but does not see that organizations and their policies are, by themselves, inhuman. Consciousness II supports the Corporate State and seeks happiness in its artificial rewards, mistakenly believing that such a state is necessary and rational in this industrial age.

These two forms of unreality, Consciousness I and II, render us powerless. We cannot act constructively so long as we are the prisoners of myth. Consciousness I exhausts its energy blaming scapegoats such as Communists, hippies, and liberals. Consciousness II offers solutions that would but strengthen existing structure. But the moment that our eyes are opened to the true causes of our self-destruction, there is hope.

What the times urgently demand, what our survival demands, is a new consciousness that will reassert rational control over the industrial system and the Corporate State, and transform them into a way of life that protects and advances human values. It is not necessary to destroy our machines or our material well-being; it is only necessary to guide them. Such a new consciousness must reject the old myths, must reject the mindless operation of the State, must reassert the reality of nature and of man's nature. Today, in this moment of most desperate need, that new consciousness is at last emerging—the spontaneous outgrowth of the fears and hopes of the new generation.

All around us today we see new ways of thinking and living: long hair, student protest, rock music, rejection of old careers. Many people find all of this shocking, frightening, senseless. But against the background of what has

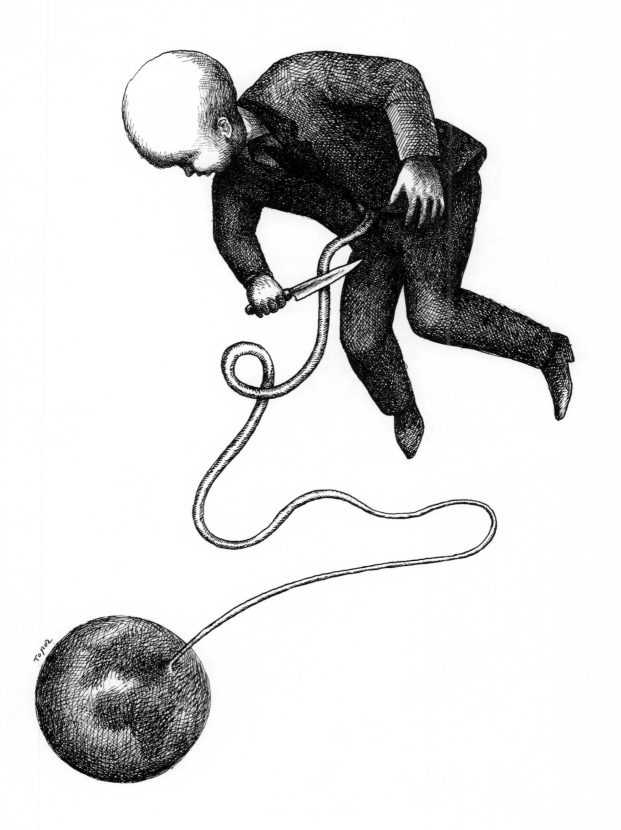

gone wrong with America, it all makes sense. There is a logic to it that explains each large and small experiment. Taken as a whole, it represents the only large-scale search for common sense and self-preservation that can be found in America today, the only major effort to come to grips with reality and thereby reassert man's control of his own fate. This is the beginning of a new consciousness, Consciousness III.

If the American Corporate State is, despite the wishes of a majority of its people, mindlessly destroying the land, culture, and people of a country in Southeast Asia, it is rational to refuse to become an instrument of that war, and to refuse obedience to laws that seek to compel a human being, despite his deepest convictions, to kill other human beings. If the State wants its citizens identically boxed and packaged, all the better to serve its rigid organizational structure, it makes sense to wear long hair and beards and clothes that constitute a refusal to be regimented. If the State wants all decisions made by remote central managers or by even more remote computers, it makes sense to insist that real people be allowed to participate in the making of decisions that affect their lives. If official language has been so debased that making war is called "making peace," and human needs are described in terms of manufactured appliances, there is a genuine need for the new language of rock music to aid in the effort to regain truth.

A revolution usually means the seizure of power by one group from another. But the revolution of the new generation is very different. It is not directed against other people, but against an impersonal system. And its objective is to place that system under the guidance of a mind—to reassert values where none are now recognized. The first stage of this revolution must be personal and cultural—the reassertion of values in each individual's life. The revolution will change the political structure of the State only as its final act. This is revolution by consciousness.

Revolution by consciousness is possible—and an orthodox revolution is not—because the Corporate State, while almost impregnable from outside, is astonishingly vulnerable from within. It is operated not by force but by willing workers and willing consumers. They have been persuaded to pursue goals set for them by the State. But if young lawyers will work only in firms that do some public service, if consumers refuse to buy the furs of endangered animal species, the State will be forced to obey, and it will begin to be turned to human ends. Opinion is not enough. People must change their working and consumer lives. And they can do this only by a rediscovery of self. It is only by a renewed self-knowledge that we can learn what work gives our lives meaning, and what material things will not impoverish us but affirm us.

Recovery of self is possible for people of all ages and conditions. The coming of revolution has started with youth, but all others can join. They need not adopt the specifics of the youth culture; a sixty-year-old person does not have to wear bellbottoms. All that he needs is to make as honest a search for his own happiness and meaning as youth are making for theirs. There need be no unnatural warfare between generations, incited by promoters of hate. Parents do not want to hate their children. And children—our children of the new generation—desperately want the support and the wisdom of older people, who have too long left it to the young to carry alone the burden of resisting the inhuman Corporate State.

The generation of Consciousness III does not seek anything alien and strange. It is the Corporate State that has turned our country into a foreign and unrecognizable land. The new consciousness dreams the old American dream—of individual fulfillment and brotherly love. It is the old dream restated in terms of the realities and the promise of a technological society, where man must understand and master his machines.

To write about the coming revolution in terms of abstract concepts like "consciousness" is to risk missing its essence. This revolution does not find expression in theories. It is expressed all around us by the bloom of renewed life. Faces are gentler and more beautiful. People are better with each other. There are more smiles, more love. There is new hope, for young people have rediscovered a future, where until recently no future could even be imagined. This is the Revolution: the rebirth of people in a sterile land.

Charles A. Reich is Professor of Law at Yale University and author of "The Greening of America."